A HISTORY OF

EASTBOURNE'S BUSES

A HISTORY OF

EASTBOURNE'S BUSES

MICK HYMANS

First published 2011

The History Press
The Mill, Brimscombe Port
Stroud, Gloucestershire, GL5 2QG
www.thehistorypress.co.uk

British Library Cataloguing in Publication Data.
A catalogue record for this book is available from the British Library.

ISBN 978 0 7524 5803 8

Typesetting and origination by The History Press
Printed in Great Britain
Manufacturing managed by Jellyfish Print Solutions Ltd

Contents

Introduction

I ventured into the bus depot in Churchdale Road one Saturday morning in September 1972 looking for a job. It was supposed to be a temporary position as I had just heard I'd passed my accountancy exams, had handed in my notice at the dead-end office job I had been working in and had not yet found the wonderful new job I was looking for. Why the bus depot? Well my father had been a bus driver there in the sixties and he seemed to have enjoyed his time there.

I was told I could start as a conductor the following Monday and as I was twenty years old that was perfect, as their rules stated that after six months as a conductor they would train me to be a driver and that would be just after my twenty-first birthday. I duly passed my test first time, much to the surprise and delight of my instructor!

Little did I think that thirty-eight years later I would still be there! Why did I stay? Well I found out that the other platform staff were true friends (not colleagues who would gladly stab you in the back for promotion to the next rung up the corporate ladder), the wages were far better than I had been earning and it was enjoyable – if you think the programme *On the Buses* was amusing, it was nowhere near as funny as the real thing. Copious amounts of alcohol consumed at the Archery Tavern near the depot probably had a bearing on this!

Unfortunately the advent of one-man-operated buses put an end to most of the tomfoolery, but by that time, I was married with a mortgage that needed paying and the idea of going back to a career in accountancy was a non-starter.

Many a time I heard someone at the depot say 'You could write a book about this place' and I agreed, so I set about writing one. Much has been written about the buses themselves from people far more knowledgeable about the technical aspects; I was more interested in the operational side, how the social changes of the last century affected the services and the human-interest stories that occurred throughout its history. I have been chairman of the Union branch at the depot for about the last twenty years and this has given me a greater insight into the problems of running a bus company.

I must thank the contributors of the photographs, the librarians at Eastbourne Central Library for their assistance, Beckett Newspapers for allowing me to use articles from their publications, the management of Eastbourne Buses Ltd for unrestricted access to their archives, and my long-suffering girlfriend Lynne who had to look at the back of my head for hours on end while I sat in the corner of the lounge typing this using one finger!

Mick Hymans

Chapter 1

The First Years

*Act of Parliament; trolleybuses versus buses; complaints; accidents; expansion;
steam-powered buses; byelaws*

The Forerunners

The oldest record of public transport I can find in Eastbourne is a stagecoach that ran a daily
service, except Sundays, between Eastbourne and London in 1795. A few years later in 1829 a
stage used to run from Brighton to Hastings via Eastbourne. This was operated by The Spread
Eagle Coach Company with a coach called *The Wonder*. The fare was a massive 6s for an inside
seat or 3s for an outside seat. Luggage was charged at 4s 6d per cwt. Another company called
Crosweller Breeds & Co. was charging 12s and 6s respectively for the same journey in their
coach called *The Hero*. These would have been very expensive at the time and must have been
accessible only by the well-to-do, rather than the masses.

Locally a company called Chapman & Sons were operating horse-drawn buses from
the 1870s. In 1884 a private company applied to be able to build and run a tramway from
Eastbourne to the village of Pevensey, about 5 miles to the east. Eastbourne Corporation was
successful in their opposition to this.

Another scheme was put forward four years later, which revived the idea of a tramway to
Pevensey as well as a network of tram routes within the town. Again the local opposition to this
was successful.

In 1902 Mr G.S. Prismall applied for a licence to run motorbuses in Eastbourne, but his
application was not granted.

1903

It is a well-documented fact that Eastbourne had the first Municipal Motor Omnibus Operated
Bus Company in the world. It was empowered by Parliament via the Eastbourne Corporation
Act to own and run motor vehicles. This Act gave the Corporation sole rights to run motorbuses within, and 1 mile beyond, the borough boundary. Routes and fares were regulated by
the Board of Trade. The Corporation could only run buses along certain roads within the borough, and the Board of Trade had to be consulted before any routes could be changed.

The committee of the Eastbourne Corporation charged with running the bus services was
the Electric Light Committee. The members carefully investigated the merits of different buses
available at the time. A firm called the Stirling Motor Carriage Company Ltd were producing

three various petrol-engined buses from twelve- to twenty-two-seaters ranging from £683 to £810 each. Members of this committee travelled to London to trial one of these on the route from Oxford Circus to Cricklewood.

Milnes-Daimler, a German manufacturer, offered a choice of five buses. Their largest bus could carry thirty-two passengers and cost £900. Again members trialled one of these in London and also in Hastings.

An electric bus was also considered. This was produced by the City and Suburban Electric Carriage Company, and could carry sixteen passengers, two of whom sat alongside the driver. Before any could be ordered, their specification was changed to a vehicle running on a combination of a petrol engine and electric power. The petrol engine would charge the accumulator batteries via a dynamo. This stored power was to assist on gradients and for running short journeys unaided. The committee decided to trial a smaller six-seater Phaeton and were pleased with the smoothness of starting and lack of vibration.

The committee resolved to trial two Milnes-Daimler vehicles of differing sizes, fourteen- and thirty-two-seaters, for a week at a sum not exceeding £15.

The first bus ran on 12 April 1903 from Eastbourne Station to an affluent area called Meads, which was built mainly of large Victorian mansions where the residents enjoyed the luxury of servants. The service ran via Terminus Road and the seafront, returning via Meads Road and Grove Road. The bus used was a single-deck Milnes-Daimler.

The buses were originally kept in a yard at Junction Road but were soon to move to rented premises in Firle Road nearer the east end of town.

It only took two weeks for the first complaint about the service to appear in the *Eastbourne Chronicle*. The correspondent, a resident of Meads, stated that the new omnibus should not be able to go so fast downhill, adding that:

> When I rode on it into town after it had passed St John's Road it seemed to take a sudden plunge down the decline and rushed past the next road at what I should say was quite 20mph (and many years of experience of bicycling has made me a fair judge of speed). Half-way down a cart horse shied and if it had swerved across the road there would have been an

One of the original Milnes-Daimler buses in Meads Street. Life must have been fairly easy for the conductor, with a maximum of fourteen passengers. (Eastbourne Buses Ltd)

accident, as the road was too narrow and the pace too fast to prevent such a heavy car from avoiding it. We tore round the corner of Carlisle Road at increased speed only just avoiding a heavy water cart. If private motorists choose to risk their necks, the driver of a public motorcar is hardly justified in endangering the lives of passengers. The great object seems to be the making of as many journeys in the day as possible. Perhaps this may be advisable in the view of the smash-up which seems to be impending and which will probably put an end to all journeys on the part of the bus and any luckless passenger in it at the time.

This was the first, but by no means the last, letter of complaint to be printed in the local press. In the same edition, however, there was a more positive letter from a passenger who was quite impressed with the comfort and smoothness of running of a Milnes-Daimler.

On 1 May a special meeting of the Town Council was held to consider reports on the provision of motor omnibuses. The Electric Light Committee applauded the full council's decision to establish a motorbus service and recommended they purchase top-seated buses. The chairman, Cllr Maude, said that the committee favoured buses with outside seats, although personally he was not in favour. He also stated that he was sorry that an electric bus was not available that would meet their requirements. He proposed that four Milnes-Daimler type be purchased. This was seconded by Cllr Breach.

However, all was not plain sailing. Cllr Eden put forward an amendment that six buses be purchased – three open-top and three single closed-tops. Alderman Keay objected to this increased outlay, saying that designs were improving all the time and they could be left with an obsolete fleet. He also stated that 'when stationary there was a large amount of vibration whilst the olfactory nerve was somewhat offended by the petrol'. He went on to state that sooner or later they would have an electric bus and steam buses would be substantially improved.

Cllr Maude then chipped in again to state that he thought the larger steam buses would create more wear on the roads and we did not have roads made from wooden blocks like Hastings who were running steam buses. He also thought that smaller, but more frequent buses would make for a better service. (Isn't it strange that this debate is still going on over 100 years later?)

The class society then showed itself when Cllr Wenham strongly advocated open-top buses but said if the aristocratic districts preferred closed vehicles he had no objection to them having such, provided they did not hereafter lay claim to the top-seated buses which the poorer east end would prefer in all cases and which he was confident would be the more generally popular.

Timetables and fare charts for the first two routes in Eastbourne. (Eastbourne Buses Ltd)

It was then stated that no buses with outside seats could be delivered before October.

Cllr Sharp then said that he thought that the purchase of two buses would be ample and was not sure that even only having two would return a profit. He also said he did not like the thought of money being spent in Germany and felt the buses should be sourced from Birmingham or London.

Cllr Wright then stated that he thought the council should buy five buses, so one could be held in reserve.

Cllr Simmons then threw the meeting into disarray by proposing that Messrs Chapman & Sons should be given the option of running the new service. He went on to say that he had it in writing that they would be willing to supply and run a motor omnibus service to the satisfaction of the council. His motion was defeated by a large majority. Simmons then put forward another amendment that the town buy four Milnes-Daimlers (two open-seated and two closed) and one of Clarkeson's steam motorbuses. Cllr Wenham seconded this. This amendment was narrowly defeated thirteen votes to fifteen.

The original motion that four buses be purchased was voted on and after more discussion this motion was passed by eighteen votes to ten. Now you might think that that would have been an end to it, but no!

Alderman Keay put forward another amendment saying that before they were ordered, the Electric Light Committee should report on the advisability of substituting Clarkeson's Steam Buses or buses of some other maker. Councillors complained that this motion was out of order, but they were overruled by the Mayor and this amendment was also passed.

So basically, after all that it was left to the Electric Light Committee to buy four buses of their choice. These were to be financed by a loan taken out by the council over an eight-year period, so the new buses had to survive for at least eight years. Four Milnes-Daimlers were purchased for £3,000.

By June the service was running with two single-deck buses and the first letter complaining there were not enough buses and that the fares were too high had appeared in the local paper. Some things never change!

Two weeks later at the next committee meeting it was stated that 7,470 passengers had been taken on the Seaside route and 4,555 on the Meads run. A total mileage of 1,446 had been completed and £85 5s 3d taken.

A letter was read from Messrs Chapman & Sons offering to sell their plant to the council. This offer was declined. Letters between Mr Chapman and the council appeared in the paper with Mr Chapman complaining that he had been hard done by, but his complaints seemed to fall on deaf ears.

Plans were approved for a new shed at Roselands in the east end of town at a cost of £950. In June, a Clarkeson's steam bus was trialled in Eastbourne. The vehicle brought to Eastbourne was a small tourist-type vehicle that only carried six passengers, but was sent to demonstrate the principle of the mechanism. It proved to be perfectly smooth, especially when starting or stopping, and was free from vibration. It was fuelled by a paraffin burner placed in the front of the bus that heated water from tanks situated beneath the passenger seats. The only gas that could be seen escaping from the vehicle was a little water vapour. The bus had a range of 120 miles. Windows fitted to the sides were hinged halfway up so could be folded down for ventilation. There was no need to oil any moving parts as they all ran through an oil bath and this only had to be changed every 1,000 miles. One drawback of this design was that their largest vehicle could only carry fourteen passengers.

The committee were invited to send a small delegation to the German firm of Durkopp in order to see what buses they could offer and to travel on them to assess suitability. The accounts for the year ending March 1904 show that £10 was paid for the hire of a Durkopp bus, and this

The first three Milnes-Daimler buses, purchased 1903, pictured in the yard in Junction Road with the London, Brighton & South Coast Railway gantry and trucks behind them. (Eastbourne Buses Ltd)

appeared on the streets of Eastbourne in August. The option to buy the bus for £660 was not taken up.

A gentleman in the local press in August 1903 stated that, in his opinion, until the roads were improved, the buses would never take the strain. He went on to say 'if motors have come to stay, we must have wood-paved streets. There are some people, it is often said, who require a good shaking. Let them get into a motor and take a trip down Seaside and they will have it.' He then went on to state that trams would be better and that in time the authorities would see their mistake in opting for buses.

Also in August, an enterprising businessman asked if the Corporation would accept a tender to allow him to advertise on the insides of the buses. The less-than-enterprising council turned him down!

During August a sub-committee made a visit to Clarkeson's works at Chelmsford where buses were seen under construction. They were told that a fourteen-seater with the same body and upholstery as a Milnes-Daimler would cost £625, or if one finished with fourteen coats of paint and superior upholstery was required this would cost a further £23. A charabanc-style bus would cost £582 and delivery could be made in twelve weeks. The committee stated that they were not prepared to buy a double-deck bus and ordered a single-decker for £625 and stated the purchase of this bus was to be one of the original four envisaged. The aluminium body was to be varnished rather than painted and the windows were to be of the drop-down type. It cost £664.

Letters were published in the *Eastbourne Chronicle* on 22 August complaining about the bus service. There were still only two buses running and frequently one of these was not in service but being repaired, leaving parts of the town with no service. Chapman's had told the council they no longer intended running after 29 August. This meant that if only one bus was on the road a maximum of fourteen residents could be travelling at any one time. The Editor printed three letters on the subject but added that several other letters were crowded out. It is obvious that the first few months of municipal bus operation was not at all reliable and verging on farcical.

A Mr Allcock paid to have handbills printed and distributed to call a public meeting. The meeting was held in the recreation ground in Seaside in the poorer east end of the town and 1,500 people attended. Mr Allcock, who had previously handed in a petition to the council measuring over 47ft long with over 1,000 signatures demanding a tram system, addressed the meeting stating at the outset that the costs incurred by him arranging the meeting amounted to 18s 6d and there would be a collection to help with his costs. The meeting, which was very well-reported, was lively and raucous.

The problems with the bus service were discussed, one of the main issues being the cost and rapid wear of tyres. Tyres cost £90 a set and four sets per year were needed. £360 was a big outlay and it seems that spares were not stocked, so any problem with a tyre meant the bus was off the road for a while.

Alderman Wenham then addressed the meeting stating that as a member of the Electric Light Committee he had to go along with the majority decision, but personally he was in favour of trams. He also derided the type of buses already purchased, preferring open-seat buses, and called the present buses 'a cross between a sanatorium bus and a St John Ambulance.'

After a lot more discussion a resolution was passed that a tram system be installed in Eastbourne as this would be more reliable and capable of carrying more passengers than the present bus service. Part of the reason that the Corporation had purchased the Electric Light Company was to supply the tram system with power. A deputation would be sent to meet the council to put forward the views of the meeting.

By the end of the meeting £1 4s 3d had been collected so about 6s was donated to the local Leaf Homeopathic Hospital.

That meeting was held in September. An eight-man deputation led by Mr Allcock addressed the council. He stated that the residents who lived in the east end of town felt like forgotten citizens. When the town only had two buses and one broke down, their bus had been taken to keep the Meads service running. He did concede, however, that the service had improved with the arrival of new buses. He then went on to make the point that councillors had claimed that the bus service was paying, and if this was the case on vehicles that could only carry sixteen, then imagine the profit that could be made with trams capable of carrying up to seventy passengers. He implored the councillors to go on a fact-finding mission to a town that ran trams confident in the fact they would come back suitably impressed. The council stated that they had already made significant investment in buses and this could not be wasted. Not to be outdone Cllr Wenham stated that Brighton had made a £4,000 profit from their tram system and that the buses Eastbourne had bought could be used as feeders to the tram system until they were worn out and that would probably not be very long.

A vote was taken and the motion to introduce trams to Eastbourne was lost by seventeen votes to nine.

I believe that some councillors had been against the installation of a tram system, because they thought it would lower the tone and spoil the elegant lines of the town with the overhead wires and street furniture needed. Bournemouth was a similar upmarket seaside resort, which had a tram system. An article in the *Bournemouth Directory* stated that due to the disruption of laying the tracks there had been some loss of trade and visitors had been driven away, but since the works were finished, the comfort and convenience of the tramway service had banished the recollections of the troubles and the prejudice of the 'carriage people' had all but died out. Passenger loadings were about 40,000 per day and receipts were averaging £1,000 per week. The only complaints had been of noise made by the early-morning and late-evening services. Not only were the services used by workmen and for general commercial purposes, but also they were especially appreciated by the visitors and what may be called 'the classes' who enjoyed the comfortable and luxurious cars. However, we were never to find out how successful they would have been in Eastbourne.

On 1 September W. Chapman wrote to the paper complaining he had been forced to give up running his horse-drawn buses except for one route between Upperton and the Grand Hotel, which his customers had implored him to keep going. His horses and carriages were sold by auction. His horses raised 576 guineas. Six horse-drawn carriages realised 84 guineas.

Although many people sympathised with Mr Chapman, this was not universally the case. A letter appeared in October's press slating the service that Chapman's offered. The writer said that the Corporation only considered operating buses themselves because Chapman's service was so bad. He had the option of buying motorbuses, but had insisted on keeping his old rattling horse-drawn coaches. He also made the point that when Chapman had been forced to drop his fares to compete with the new buses, his buses were fuller and most of the time he was only competing against one motorbus. He also finished by asking 'were the British Museum notified of the prehistoric specimens of vehicles which were given away at less than £10 each to enrich the antiquities of Bungalow Town, Shoreham'!

The first of many bus conductors appeared before the courts in September accused of defrauding the Corporation. He had been employed as a conductor for eleven weeks, having previously had a good record with Messrs Chapman where he had worked for four years. He pleaded guilty to two charges of stealing a total of 13s 7d. He did this by falsifying his waybill and issuing 1d bell punch tickets for 2d fares. Although the court said it was being lenient, the culprit was sentenced to a second division gaol (where he was not subjected to hard labour or 'bad people'!) for fourteen days. Strangely, in those days if a conductor finished his duty after the Borough Accountant's office had closed, his takings had to be left in a box in the police station until the following morning when it was picked up.

Another letter of complaint was published from a visitor from London. On two occasions he tried to hail a bus to stop, but it sailed straight past. He found a policeman and complained to him. The copper informed him that there were proper stopping places and pointed out a small label on a lamppost which told the fact. He ended by stating 'I was thankful I lived in London, where in spite of all the heavy traffic, one can get locomotion without all these restrictions.'

During November two collisions took place with buses. Neither of these were the fault of the bus drivers.

On 18 November it was reported in the local paper that the new Clarkson Steam Motor Bus was not now expected until the end of the following month. One had recently been delivered to Torquay. It had been well-received by the public, being both quiet and smooth. It had twin rubber tyres with sprung leather seats. A poem had even been penned in its honour:

Excelsi-bus

Oh! Have you seen the motorbus?
All painted apple green
So elegant a motorbus
There surely ne'er was seen
Of every burgess 'tis the pride
To plonk his tuppence down
And go to Chelston for a ride
When he should be in town.

The shares are at a premium –
A dolt he seems to us
Who says that Dolt-er trams will come
And smash our motorbus!
So come with me and gaily glide
Without the slightest fuss
There's room for fourteen folk inside
Our giddy motorbus.

By December, there were still two pressing problems. One was still the cost and rapid wear of the solid tyres. The two Peters tyres on the driving wheels of bus No.1 had failed. The agents had replaced one and the other was in their hands. These tyres were supposed to be superior to the Turner's tyres previously used, cost £16 more but came with a guarantee. It was mentioned at a subsequent meeting that tyre protectors were available and the use of these should be looked into, but there are no details on these protectors. I presume that being kept out in the open was having a detrimental effect on them and these protectors would be covers that protected them from the elements when not in use.

The other problem was that they still needed a better depot for the fleet. Although a decision had been taken to build a shed in the Roselands (east end) area, at the time premises were being rented in Firle Road but these would soon be inadequate. Cllr Simmons on the committee had recently bought some stables in Commercial Road, near the town centre, and had offered to rent these to the Corporation with an option to buy. There would need to be some minor alterations to the premises, but he was willing to carry these out. Other premises had also been offered at the rear of Avondale Road near the east end, as well as two smaller sites. A debate ensued with the Commercial Road site being the favoured option, but some members stated they thought the purchase would be very short-sighted, as there would be no room for expansion. It was decided that the entire council should visit the site.

The meeting took place and various views were put forward, ranging from security of the site to whether it was only being considered because it was being offered by a councillor as it had no other merit, being more expensive than building their own premises and too small.

Cllr Simmons left the meeting when it came to the vote as he had a vested interest and the motion to move there was lost by a single vote. It was decided to press on with the depot at Roselands.

Politicians seem to have been mistrusted as much then as they are today. Cllr Simmons had come under a certain amount of criticism as to his motive of buying the stables and then trying to rent them to the Corporation. An article in the paper sprang to his defence under the heading 'A Plea For Fair Play', stating that the truth should be told. The premises had come up for public auction and been won fairly by Cllr Simmons who was well-pleased with his purchase. He had not offered it to the Corporation himself, but had been approached by the Mayor and had actually then offered it for rent at under the market value. Those councillors who voted in favour of it did so in the interests of efficiency and economy, rather than loyalty to a fellow councillor.

1904

Two days into 1904 the Electric Light Committee met and heard details of a Clarkeson's double-decker costing £807 which they hoped they could deliver by May, but stated that the delivery date for one already on order had to be put back to February due to slow delivery of materials. They decided the chairman and electrical engineer should go to Torquay to see one running there.

At the first full council meeting a week later, this trip to Torquay was cancelled as a waste of money as they said one had already been inspected in Chelmsford, thus ruining another jolly at the ratepayers' expense!

The Mayor decided that the whole question of premises could be discussed again, where after much debate it was decided to look for other alternative premises.

Also at this meeting, some councillors were surprised to find out that the management of the bus service had been transferred to the Borough Accountant, Mr John Allcock, but were told that this had been decided at a previous meeting. Allcock was told to revise the bus timings with a view to lessening the rate of speed, but reported back to a later meeting that he would not alter the timetables as this would lead to some disappointment to the public.

The first bus driver to be prosecuted was a William Billington. He was brought before the Mayor and another magistrate for driving on New Year's Eve with no front light whilst driving from Old Town to the town centre. A policeman noticed this and tried to stop him. When asked why he did not stop for the policeman, he replied that he was not allowed to stop between authorised stopping places! He was fined 6s.

At the end of January, the Motor Bus Sub-Committee was given powers to buy two new buses. It was also decided that the name of the route be painted on the front of the buses.

The committee then made a recommendation to the full council that four new buses were purchased. They could choose from:

Clarkeson single-deck (Delivery in July)	£735
Clarkeson double-deck (Delivery in August)	£897
Milnes-Daimler single-deck (Delivery in April)	£825
Milnes-Daimler double-deck (Delivery in June)	£900

When this came before the council, amendments were put that four double-deckers be bought. Other councillors thought that these doubles would be harder on their tyres; however the Electric Light Committee's recommendations won the day.

The residents of the east end wanted the route extended to an area of the town known as Norway, which was only ½ mile at the most past the terminal point of the Archery Tavern. Surveys were carried out which showed that on average only four passengers boarded at the Archery and only three alighted, and that running times would not allow the extension of the route. So the poor residents had to continue walking to catch their bus, and invariably see the bus leave for town even though they had hailed the bus and the conductor had spotted them.

More derogatory letters appeared in the local press, including one which said it would be better if the buses were taken off the road completely, so people could walk to their destination rather than wait in vain at a bus stop for 20 minutes and then have to walk because there was no sign of the bus.

One of the Clarkeson's steam buses that proved to be quieter and smoother but succumbed to Eastbourne's chalky hard water within three years. (Eastbourne Buses Ltd)

In April the accounts were published which covered the period from the start of the service until 31 December 1903. They showed that 294,922 passengers had been carried over 36,800 miles with their four buses that had been introduced at various times during the year. It cost just over 1s per mile to run a bus, which worked out to £17 9s per week per bus. The cost of tyres warranted a mention – these worked out to 4d per mile. After all the expenses were taken into account the Corporation made a profit of £67 3s 11d.

It was decided that tyres for the new Milnes-Daimler on order should be purchased direct from the manufacturers, thereby saving £37.

A representative from Clarkeson's also visited Eastbourne and stated that they were working the buses too much as 'they were of such delicate construction, that they should only be run five days a week, so that their insides could be well greased once a week.'

In May it was suggested that buses should run along the seafront. This led to some dissent among members of the council. In the past, private operators had been refused permission to run along the promenade. Inhabitants of Grand Parade petitioned the council complaining about the increase in noise. One councillor said they should not be competing with the private operators on the seafront. This argument was rebutted by another speaker who said that was exactly the reason they were operating and to keep them off the seafront when the demand was so great would be absurd. Alderman Wenham applauded the proposal and said 'it broke through the snobbish idea that the parades were to be kept scrupulously select'. The committee overwhelmingly voted in favour of running buses along the promenade.

Concern was raised that the steam bus had been out on a Sunday and the driver had applied to be paid for his labours. During the discussion, the committee were accused of using it for Sunday rides out, which they denied. It was then stated that the bus had been sent out on trial trips. The response to this was that any work and testing should be done at night and a fitter should be employed overnight. The committee decided that it could go out on Sundays even though they had been accused of Sunday trading.

The new shed at Roselands was still the favoured option, but the cost of this had risen to £1,400.

Although there were still letters of complaint in the paper, the Corporation were not the only public transport in the town to run into trouble. Up before the courts was a Mr James Edwards who had been summoned before the court for being drunk in charge of a horse and carriage. He pleaded not guilty. Mrs Emily Agnes Hamilton told the court that she and her three friends had ordered the cab to take them home from a Primrose League meeting at Devonshire Park. The trip home was very jerky sometimes going very fast and then slowly. When they spoke to him about his erratic driving, it became evident that he was very drunk. They all alighted the carriage at the first lady's home, and the other three walked home, as they were too frightened to stay in the carriage. Mrs Beale, another passenger, told the court he was weaving from side to side and was constantly beating his horse. The defendant called three witnesses, including his employer, who stated that they had been with the defendant during the course of the evening and all vouched for his sobriety. The defendant's employer stated that the reason for the ladies' trouble was that the horse was blind! The chairman stated that they all knew from experience of driving a blind horse that they weave from side to side. They chastised the owner for sending out such a horse and gave the driver an absolute discharge.

One who was not so lucky was steam bus driver Mr William Rowe, who found himself before the court for speeding. He was accused of driving through Terminus Road at a dangerous pace. He also pleaded not guilty. PC Morris stated that he was on duty at the station point when he saw 'the number 2 steam bus come along Terminus Road at a tremendous pace – quite 12 miles an hour.' The driver told the court that the bus was under proper control and denied going that fast as he had just started after making frequent stops in Terminus Road. He also stated that it was a new bus and the machinery was making more noise than usual so gave the impression of speed. When asked what his wages were, he declared 30s per week plus a bonus of 2s 6d if he ran without smoke. He also stated that he worked from 7.10 in the morning till 10 in the evening with an hour each for dinner and tea. He also had two evenings off a week.

The Chief Constable said they had not only received complaints from the public about excessive speed, but from the Electric Light Committee themselves.

The chairman of the bench said he would treat him the same as if he was driving a private motorcar, fined him £2 and costs and endorsed his licence. He also told the defendant he must be guided by his own eyes and common sense. William must have been a fairly feisty character as he then asked the chairman what he should do if he was driving with common sense and the police stopped him again. The chairman said that whenever the police told the defendant to stop, he must do it.

The committee accepted an offer by Milnes-Daimler to supply a top-seater rather than the single ordered. This offer was accepted.

In June the company first published their timetable in the *Eastbourne Chronicle*. This timetable was updated on a monthly basis. The first timetable showed that three routes were being run with the first bus starting from the town to go to Meads at 7.45a.m., with the last leaving the town centre for the east end at 10.05p.m. Details of fares and stopping places were also given.

By July, the bus service along the seafront had begun and was very successful. Too successful for some people, in fact. Another letter appearing in the paper complained of overloading. It was claimed by the correspondent that:

Four, if not five, adults were allowed to stand down the centre of the bus and some on the platform outside. The seats, both inside and on the top, were of course, quite full. The conductor, on being spoken to said they had no rules as to the number of passengers to be carried and they did their best not to overload going uphill as the bus would not move.

It is interesting to note that few contributors to the letters columns used their own names. The previous letter was just attributed to 'A resident' while another letter in the same edition accusing the buses of being dangerous, unreliable and a stinking nuisance signed himself as 'One Who Detests Petrol'.

Although the poorer classes in the town were beginning to appreciate the bus service, many residents of the classier areas were not. Apart from the residents of Grand Parade who had protested about a new service, complaints were received about buses running too early, stating that 9 o'clock was early enough for buses to start.

Residents in Upperton Road were always complaining about something. Earlier in the year they moaned that the destination boards on the buses stated they terminated at the 'Cemetery'. They complained about this, saying that they went to the cemetery so often they had nicknamed the buses 'hearses'. They thought a destination of 'Upperton' would be more suitable to the area. They were successful with their complaint. They then complained that Upperton Road was not a suitable road to run motorbuses, although it was a wide main thoroughfare into town, and presented a petition organised by a Col Cardwell to the council asking for the service to be withdrawn and replaced by horse-drawn vehicles. They accused the new motorbuses of being noisy, evil-smelling and dust-raising, saying that visitors and residents alike were being driven away by these motorbuses and that the number of houses that had fallen empty in their neighbourhood was sufficient proof that the buses were not appreciated and that they were driving all the better class of people away.

The petition was considered by the committee and it was decided that Col Cardwell be informed that the buses along Upperton Road to Old Town would be diverted via Water Lane (now called Southfields Avenue) if the Board of Trade agreed and that the Corporation had no powers to run horse-drawn buses.

Residents in Water Lane then raised a petition against running buses along their lane, protesting that Upperton Road was much wider than Water Lane, so the nuisance of noise and fumes would be worse for them.

A Board of Trade Inspector subsequently held a meeting in the waiting room of the Town Hall, where lengthy submissions were put from both sides. The inspector reported back to the Board of Trade who subsequently denied the Corporation permission to run along Water Lane.

By July the new route along the seafront was proving to be the most profitable. From 25 June to 18 July, £140 had been taken, whereas £122 taken on the Upperton route, £120 on the Old Town route and only £65 on the Meads route.

The erection of a new bus shed was gathering pace. A tender for £1,722 had been accepted from Mr Joseph Martin, being the cheapest of nine bids received. Cllr Climpson wanted to know why the price had increased so much from the original quotes and expected the front to 'be lined in gold' at that price. He was informed that the first estimate had been for a shed housing six buses but this had now been revised for a building that housed twelve.

It was decided to press on as quickly as possible as three buses were being stored outside overnight and it was duly built for the tendered price of £1,722.

In August, another bus driver, Harry Key, was in court accused of speeding in a steam bus on the Meads route. He had been spotted by a policeman who claimed he was going at about 15mph downhill around the bend at Carlisle Road. He also had a witness to this. The bus driver objected to the witness as he had been involved in a previous accident with him and declared he thought the witness had a grudge against him. The witness denied any grudge. The driver also objected to the fact he was unable to get passengers as witnesses as he had no idea of the alleged offence until an hour after it occurred so only had his conductor to speak for him. He then told the bench that in his opinion it should be left to the driver to determine what was a safe speed. The bench disagreed! They then asked him if there were any occasions where he thought that travelling over 12mph was acceptable. The defendant said he did not wish to say that and said that 12mph was a safe pace if the road was clear. He confirmed that he was given enough time to run the route and that he never left the station early, although time-keeping was the responsibility of the conductor who went by the Town Hall clock. He went on to say that when appointed he was never told of any speed limits.

His conductor stated that the bus was not going at the pace alleged and said that he had been able to jump off the bus and run forward to mount the front of the bus to collect the fares of two passengers seated with the driver. He said the bus was full and he had the 'bus full' board showing at the time and in his view they were travelling at 9 or 10mph. The constable said that he had seen the conductor do this, but this had been after the bus had passed him. When questioned as to why if he was full he was not carrying standing passengers, he said he had been instructed not to because the bus was very shaky due to a couple of loose bolts!

The Traffic Manager, Mr Smith, was then called to give evidence. In reply to questions he said that passengers were given about 10 inches of seating space each, but they do carry one or two more at their own risk. He went on to say it was difficult to keep passengers from getting on and overloading the bus. He admitted that a verbal warning about the state of the bus had been given to staff a few days previously, but nothing on that day. He went on to state that whilst cab drivers were legally bound not to overload their cabs, there was no rule against buses doing so.

The magistrate summed up by saying that he was in no doubt the bus was speeding and that 8 or 9mph was sufficient in any circumstances for a bus to travel, adding that driving at anything approaching 12mph would endanger the public. He fined the driver £2 with 16s costs and asked the driver if he would be paying. Driver Key said he did not know whether he had to pay or if the Corporation would pay the fine. Mr Allcock (the Borough Accountant) who had been watching the proceedings shook his head at the suggestion that the Corporation should pay the penalty. At a subsequent meeting however it was decided that the Corporation pay half of Driver Key's fine and pay all his costs.

The above case prompted the Electric Light Committee to draw up some byelaws to be submitted to the council for approval. These included:

– No passenger shall play any musical instrument or smoke any tobacco inside any motor omnibus.

– A person suffering from intoxication, or affected by any infectious or contagious disease, shall not enter any omnibus or if any person is found to be so on the bus, they can be asked to leave or removed under the direction of the driver or conductor.

– No person shall swear or use abusive language, commit any nuisance or interfere with any passenger.

– No person shall spit on the floor, platform, side, roof or cushions.

– The conductor may refuse a person whose dress or clothing may soil the bus or other passengers' entry. Any person already on the bus with soiled clothing may be asked to leave and have his fare returned.

– Personal luggage not exceeding 28lb may be carried. The conductor may refuse any luggage that may annoy or inconvenience any passenger.

– No passenger shall travel on the platform or steps or stand on the top deck or interior of any bus.

– When a bus is full, no passenger may attempt to enter the bus and must leave if asked to do so by the conductor. When the bus is full a conspicuous notice must be placed in a conspicuous place on the bus.

– No person shall enter, or attempt to enter, mount or leave the bus while it is in motion. No dogs are to be carried on or in the bus.

– Any person offending against or committing a breach of these regulations shall be liable to a fine not exceeding forty shillings.

Cllr Climpson also asked if there are any laws against speeding. The Town Clerk informed him that drivers must not drive recklessly or carelessly to the danger of the public and that, as Parliament did not think a speeding law was necessary, there was no need for a separate byelaw.

A rule was introduced, purportedly in the interests of 'safety', banning ladies from sitting on the front seat with the driver. It was also suggested that lampposts on bus routes should have red bands painted around them to aid visibility.

The Traffic Manager stated that he was making good improvements since his appointment and two or three buses that had been in a deplorable state had been thoroughly done up and it was hoped to do up the others at an early date. He went on to state that if they were to be ready for the 1905 season, they would need another two open-top buses. The council were recommended to agree to the purchase of two more Milnes-Daimler open-top buses.

He also asked that he should be able to buy a bicycle. Cllr Hoadley asked why he should need one when he had the opportunity to travel by bus. Cllr Simmons said it was necessary that he had the opportunity to travel quickly without relying on the buses and he was given permission to purchase a bicycle.

A local jeweller, W. Bruford, had an offer of £5 accepted to be able to advertise on the back of 250,000 2d tickets.

There seems to have been an extraordinary amount of accidents, bearing in mind the number of buses and lack of traffic on the roads. Damages of £1 18s were paid for damage to a hand truck and 5s were paid to its owner for personal injury.

A page from the official accounts in 1904. (Eastbourne Buses Ltd)

Poor driver Harry Key was having a torrid year. Not only had he been prosecuted for speeding, but he was also involved in an accident with a horse-drawn Victoria carriage near the railway station. This time, however, he was not the defendant. It appears that the carriage, being driven by a Mr Hunnisett, was on the wrong side of the road and the collision occurred as the bus turned the corner out of Ivy Terrace. Considerable damage was done to the carriage and the poor passenger, a Miss Bockett, was thrown clear and landed on the road, suffering a head injury that knocked her unconscious.

In court her solicitor argued that it was the bus driver's fault as buses invariably drove down the middle of the road, intimating that because the Corporation owned them, the drivers thought it was fine to do so. Harry Key said they did sometimes keep out further than car drivers due to the camber of the road, but in this instance the road was fairly narrow so he was keeping to the left.

The magistrate declared that the bus driver had three witnesses to say he was on the left and found the carriage driver guilty, fining him 1s with 11s 6d costs.

An article in the *Automotor Journal* praised the bus service in Eastbourne, with an article headed 'Triumphant Motor Buses' stating it was little short of a revelation how the general life of Eastbourne had been improved by the successful motorbus service. It continued that the

The entire fleet poses in late 1904. (Eastbourne Buses Ltd)

steadiness and ease with which these vehicles – which were invariably packed both inside and out – swept along was a triumph of self-propelled locomotion, akin to the smoothness of a tramcar running on rails.

At this time if a conductor was found to have a passenger on his bus without having paid, he was liable to a fine of a shilling. Cllr Duke thought this was not severe enough and that he should be dismissed.

In September the first double-deck Clarkeson's steam bus arrived in Eastbourne. It was taken to the Town Hall where members of the Electric Light Committee were taken for a trial trip. The bus was driven by a driver from Clarkeson's with a Corporation driver in attendance. They were driven to Hampden Park where they inspected the bus, comparing it favourably with the single-deckers already in service, but questioned whether it would stand the serious wear and tear it would be subjected to.

Another conductor, James Wernham, twenty, gave in to temptation of making some easy money, but ended up in court being charged with embezzlement. An inspector had boarded his bus on a journey to Meads and found a passenger who had had her ticket punched twice. Investigations showed that a previous conductor had issued the ticket and the defendant had picked it up from the floor, re-punched it and re-issued it. Investigation showed that he had punched 223 tickets but only 191 were missing from those issued to him, leaving a discrepancy of thirty-two tickets. The defendant stated that he had dropped his tickets on the floor and must have picked up some old tickets by mistake as well as his own tickets. A police officer said that when they had searched James, he had found a ladies' gold watch and two rings. The defendant was sentenced to twenty-one days in a second division gaol (with no hard labour).

1905

The New Year got off to a good start. The manager reported that over the Christmas holiday, they did not suffer a single breakdown. To reward their regular passengers, it was put forward that books of 1*d* and 2*d* tickets be sold and that thirteen tickets be sold for the price of twelve. They had been sent samples of similar tickets from Bournemouth and Nottingham.

There had been calls from the public to be told if a bus was not running. To do this they decided to find a tradesman in Old Town connected to the telephone who would put a notice in his window if the bus was 'off service'.

The Corporation was still criticised for its service. Over the Christmas period, special buses were put on to take theatre-goers home from the Hippodrome Theatre. The cab drivers were upset that the buses were taking trade away from them. Some of the councillors sympathised with their point of view and thought the buses should not be running at that time of night and the proceeds would not cover their costs. Cllr Climpson thought that the manager should not have introduced the service without the consent of the committee. Other councillors stated that if a private operator pulled up outside a place of entertainment and waited, they would lay themselves open to prosecution, and that the Corporation was abusing their privilege. However, the majority of the committee thought they were simply serving their customers and those patrons only willing to pay 2*d* to get home would not use the cabs, so were not greatly affecting their businesses.

It was good news for the conductors as well. It was proposed to increase their wages from £1 per week to £1 2*s* 6*d* owing to their new responsibilities and if their work was satisfactory then a further increase of 2*s* 6*d* would be earned.

One rather glaring blunder came to light though. The entrances to the new depot were not wide enough for a bus to enter! The problem arose because the architect designed the doors so the buses could be driven straight in, in which case they would fit, but in practice the buses would have to approach at an angle, so they were not wide enough.

By March 1905 the committee had had a rethink on their ban on advertising on the insides of the buses and asked the Traffic Manager to submit sketches showing the available spaces.

On 27 March the Borough Accountant reported that both steam buses were running without brakes and the drivers were stopping by reversing the engines. Both buses were immediately taken in for repairs.

A Mr Gengnagel had written asking that bus services should connect with each other in the town centre. He was told that this would be given due consideration. Why a simple idea such as this should be left up to a member of the public to come up with did not reflect well on the management of the day.

Passengers had been asking that the interiors of the vehicles should be lit. The manager informed the committee that he had studied operations in London and that acetylene lighting could be relied upon.

It was mentioned in committee that a bus had managed to go 17,183 miles without any repairs being done to it and this was a remarkable achievement.

By May, receipts and numbers of passengers had been rising steadily and the manager had asked for permission to order two more double-deckers as a matter of urgency. Enquiries had been made, but Milnes-Daimler could not supply any vehicles until October. There was, however, a splendid new English bus on the market and this was called the Leyland. The returns over the four-day Easter period amounted to £185 and the returns over the summer months could be very large indeed and these vehicles were needed, as the present fleet could not cope with the influx of visitors. Alderman Towner cautioned the manager about mixing his vehicles as he may need different machinery and engineers to maintain them and the purchase of new vehicles should be put off until Milnes-Daimler could supply them. The Mayor agreed with this point of view.

It was pointed out that the Leylands, made by Crossley, were running between Surbiton and Kew Bridge and were proving to be thoroughly reliable. The councillors present could not decide on a way forward and decided to call another meeting involving the Finance Committee and council. The Traffic Manager and the Borough Accountant visited Kingston to view the Leylands in action and reported back that they had been only been in service for six weeks and that this was not a long enough test period. The deputation had met with a representative from Milnes-Daimler after this visit and reported that they had offered to deliver two more double-deckers by March 1906 for £925 with an option for two more.

Clarkeson's meanwhile were having problems meeting with their delivery dates and the Town Clerk was told to write declining delivery of the buses on order.

It had become clear that a profit could not be made from single-deck buses due to the lack of seats, so it was suggested that they be offered for purchase to the Highways and Sanitary Authority to convert to water-carts and dustcarts. Offers were received from Isle of Wight Express Motor Syndicate, Messrs Ramsey & Co. and Metropolitan Asylums Board to purchase them but their offers were declined.

During 1904, with depreciation, the losses had amounted to nearly £1,000. To help offset these losses, the Traffic Manager proposed that the bus service be reduced for the winter months and only five buses be run during the week with an extra bus on Saturdays. This would mean the withdrawal of buses on certain routes. This recommendation was accepted and three drivers, three conductors and one washer would be given notice from October. Some of these losses had been incurred by the so-called 'early morning buses' which were run so passengers could catch the 8.30 train on Mondays and Wednesdays. A month's takings on these buses only came to 8s for three buses running twice a week and they had to take the crew's overtime out of this as it came outside their duty times.

The council continued to be bombarded with petitions from residents and traders in the town centre that buses should not be allowed to run along their roads, even though some had been sanctioned by the Board of Trade and services were already running. Some complained that the road was too wide and lined with grass where people enjoyed walking while others complained their road was too narrow. Councillors began to get frustrated that every time improvements to the service were suggested, 'These humbugging things were thrown in their way.'

There seemed to be no end to the variety of complaints. Another one was that timetables had been placed on trees. These had been secured by nails or screws. Inhabitants of Upperton described this practice as 'vandalism'. It was agreed to remove as many as possible and put them on lampposts instead.

When a complaint was investigated from a member of the public that his bus never arrived on the afternoon of 17 June, it was discovered that the crew had taken the bus out of service and driven to Hampden Park to spend the afternoon there. The service didn't run for 4 hours. Both the driver and conductor were severely reprimanded.

Another article appeared in the *Automotor Journal*. This again praised the Corporation for the services it was running and criticised those people who were hindering the expansion of the service by their selfish petitions. It also stated that if other councils had been hesitating whether to adopt buses or a tram system, they had visited Eastbourne and had been suitably impressed that the buses were serving the town well without the expense or upheaval of installing a tram system.

By July, the Traffic Manager, Mr Turner Smith, had resigned. The committee resolved to appoint Mr E. Griffiths, the engineer in charge, at £3 10s per week and that an advertisement be placed for a traffic superintendent for £2 per week, who would have control of all outside staff.

Two of the Clarkeson's steam buses needed their boiler re-tubing, which was done by Clarkeson's. They charged £44 for this, but the Corporation only offered to pay them £22.

The staff wanted to go on an outing and asked the council to pay them 5s each as they did to the town's other employees. This request was denied, as they had been paid 5s at Christmas.

The new depot had been completed by July and was built £9 under budget. In December the committee visited the depot to see how it could be extended to accommodate the four new buses on order and instructed the Borough Surveyor to submit plans and costings to include a new storeroom and toilets.

A page from the accounts in 1905 showing costs of buses. (Eastbourne Buses Ltd)

Tyre technology had improved and the tyres to be supplied with the four buses on order would be guaranteed for 10,000 miles. These tyres were to be purchased directly from the manufacturers and Milnes-Daimler would reduce the purchase price of their buses accordingly.

An incident occurred on 12 September at about 8 in the evening, which led to the death of an elderly resident, Mr Thomas Meadows Wood. It appears that the driver, Mr John Godfrey, was driving up an incline in Bedfordwell Road and the bus slipped out of gear. As the bus slowed to a halt the victim alighted to the rear, but the bus rolled back and knocked him over. He was not badly hurt and picked himself up with the help of the conductor. He refused treatment at the Princess Alice Hospital. He was asked for a statement on 1 October but said he could not be too accurate, due to the passing of time. He said that the bus had stopped in Bedfordwell Road and he asked the conductor if they had reached the stop. The conductor had alighted, gone to the front and was talking to the driver. He alighted, but the bus ran back and knocked him over. The conductor ran to his assistance and offered to take him to the hospital. He declined as he was almost home. Before walking home he said to the driver that he should not move while at a bus stop. The driver stated that he was very sorry, but the brakes would not hold.

A doctor saw the victim early the following morning, when he was found to be suffering from a severe contusion to an elbow and shock. Although the elbow healed, Mr Wood lapsed into a state of great weakness and his heart became very feeble. Although he showed signs of rallying, he never completely recovered. He became more and more feeble and eventually died of exhaustion.

Mr Griffiths, the Corporations Motor Engineer, swore that he had tested the bus that evening and given it a thorough overhaul the following day and could find no fault with it. The coroner summed up saying that he did not regard the driver as being at all criminally responsible and returned a verdict of accident or misadventure.

1906

1906 started very badly for the Corporation and Driver John Godfrey with another fatal accident. It happened to the Town Crier, a Mr Reed, who had boarded the bus in the Old Town district and had chosen to travel into town standing on the rear platform. When the bus travelled round the double bend at the junction with Water Lane, he was thrown from the bus onto the road, and his head took the full force of the landing. He was taken to the Princess Alice Hospital where he was found to have a fractured skull and he died later of his injuries. The bus involved was a Milnes-Daimler single-decker. The conductor stated he had taken his fare and then gone inside to collect more fares, returned to the rear and was reaching for his waybill when the bus swayed. He had grabbed hold of a bracket, but noticed the passenger falling past him and onto the road. He was asked if the bus accelerated round the corner and he replied that it did not and they run in neutral for as long as possible along there. A cyclist who was following the bus stated that it was going about 12mph and he had caught the bus up and was trying to overtake it! Another witness stated that two ladies boarded at the same stop as Mr Reed and one had a dog that was made to run along behind the bus. He thought Mr Reed was fussing over the dog and not paying attention. He also stated that the driver of the bus had swerved to the right before turning left causing the bus to sway and a lady passenger was nearly thrown from her seat. The driver of the bus, Mr John Godfrey, said he was going about 8mph and had the bus under control and confirmed he was in neutral.

The jury retired to consider their verdict. On returning they said that they did not hold the driver or conductor to blame but were unanimous in their belief that buses travelled too fast around the corner. A verdict of accidental death was arrived at.

At the next committee meeting, it was decided to impose a 4mph limit on the crews at this point and to impose a speed limit of 5mph on the road down from Meads, where two drivers had already been fined for speeding.

Another accident nearly occurred when a bus was reversing round a corner at the end of its journey. It was decided to equip the conductors with red flags to warn motorists of these manoeuvres. For reversing at night, they would have red lamps.

In February, at the cabmen's annual dinner, a speaker complained about the buses, saying that Eastbourne was the only town that buses were used for pleasure purposes and that was making it difficult for the 235 cabs in the town to earn a living.

Yet another Board of Trade enquiry was held as residents had complained about plans to run buses past their Victorian mansions between the town centre and the seafront via Devonshire Park. The Corporation were permitted to run on a six-month trial basis.

The engineer and a councillor had been to test a Maudslay omnibus. This bus had been thoroughly tested and performed well and they could recommend to the council the purchase of these in the future. They also put in a quote for two Milnes-Daimlers that were currently working at Hastings. The council seemed unable to make up their minds as to the vehicles to buy. Makers and specifications were constantly being altered. Doubles seemed to be in favour most of the time, but singles had to be used on some routes – they considered sending doubles to Old Town via the Lamb Inn as 'suicidal', due to the camber of the road. They also thought larger single-deckers unsuitable for this route. They did, however, decide to buy one single- and one double-decker Maudslay. The committee were told that one of this manufacturer's buses had run non-stop from Coventry to Edinburgh.

A rather strange decision was also made to remove all the seats from the top deck of one of the original doubles and to put an additional seat where the stairs were, thereby making a nineteen-seater. This was to stop passengers being upstairs when the bus went past the Lamb Inn.

The Motor Bus Committee recommended that the drivers receive four days annual leave after serving for one year. When this was heard by the full council, an amendment was put that this be increased to six, as if anyone deserved a holiday, bus drivers did. This was referred back to the Bus Committee for further discussion. When referred back, the committee decided that six days holiday should be granted but withdrew the time-and-a-half paid for bank holidays, so crews had to work at the standard rate.

During the election an increased service was run in order to cope with those wishing to vote and, indeed, a further £28 was taken on the previous week's takings. The police superintendent stated how well he thought the buses had been driven during this time and the council agreed to pay the drivers and conductors a bonus of 1s each for their efforts.

The traffic superintendent bought in reduced fares of 1d for passengers travelling between 8a.m. and 9a.m., which is strange to today's environment when cheaper fares are offered off peak.

During the early summer there had been a spate of breakdowns. This had been put down to overcrowding putting a strain on the vehicles. At the foot of Beachy Head, when buses arrived they were besieged by passengers and the conductor could not control the crowds; buses were leaving with passengers standing inside and on the roof. The committee were hoping to have a policeman on duty there to try to control matters. The new byelaws were about to be introduced and the council hoped that these would help alleviate the situation.

Problems with breakdowns and overcrowding had even made it to the House of Commons. Mr Money MP asked the Home Secretary if he was aware that a number of motor omnibuses had been licensed in spite of the fact that they were so badly constructed, they constantly broke down, they had frequently carried more passengers than they could hold and often emitted clouds of noxious vapour, and that, moreover, they were driven recklessly to the public danger and started while passengers were still descending the stairs.

Mr Gladstone replied in writing that conditions of licensing motor omnibuses were under constant review and received very careful attention. The vehicles were largely in an experimental stage, and though strict conditions with regard to public safety were already enforced, it was perhaps early as yet to require companies to correct all defects. There had been numerous prosecutions for reckless driving and many faulty vehicles had been prohibited from plying for hire. Several points, including the emission of vapours, were receiving the attention of the Commissioner of Police and his advisers.

A letter from a Mr J. Craig had been received offering £200 for the two Clarkeson's buses that were proving to be unreliable. This offer was to be for the buses as they stood, taking on all risks. It was resolved that Mr Craig be informed that they would not accept less than £300 for the buses.

Some of the topics discussed at council meetings were amazing, indeed frightening. The subject of brakes arose and the committee decided to ask Milnes-Daimler if they could do something to improve the braking system. Further, that no bus should enter service without a proper brake and that drivers should test their brakes on every journey. The Chairman of the Committee, Cllr Duke, made an amendment to the above by insisting 'a proper brake' be changed to 'two efficient brakes'. Were the drivers still really driving buses that did not have any brakes working?

It was also decided that a new post of General Manager and Engineer be created as they thought that one man should be in overall charge. The post was to be advertised at a salary of £250, payable monthly. By September, the interviews had taken place and a Mr P. Ellison had been successful and offered the post.

Two more Milnes-Daimlers had been delivered and were running satisfactorily.

Maudslay, however, were having difficulty meeting their delivery deadlines because they were having to make alterations to their specifications due to new police regulations. A letter was sent to the company saying that if the bus had not been delivered by 30 August, the council would cancel the order and sue for damages.

During September there was yet another fatal accident, when a pedestrian, Mr Alfred Wilmshurst, was knocked down and crushed beneath the wheels of a bus in the High Street, Old Town. At the inquest the following day, his wife said he had popped out about 10.15p.m. to get a beer for his supper as he occasionally did.

A witness who was sitting at the front of the bus next to the driver stated that the bus was being driven steadily and that he was about 4ft into the road when he first saw him. The driver shouted for him to get out of the way, but the bus hit him and the driver felt the front wheel go over his body. The bus stopped quickly and the victim was lying between the front and rear wheels.

The driver, Alfred Winchester, was then called and warned that if the jury came to the conclusion he was driving carelessly, he could be tried for manslaughter. Under questioning, he said that he was only going at about 6mph, although the bus was capable of going at over 10mph at that point. He was on time and had no reason to be rushing. The first time he saw the deceased was when he walked out of the Prince Albert public house holding a beer bottle.

The coroner then stated that if a pedestrian did not get out of the way of a bus, then it was up to the bus driver to get out of the way of the pedestrian, and if the driver did not, he was responsible for their deaths, no matter how drunk or stupid they may be.

Driver Winchester said he did try to avoid him and braked hard.

The coroner said it was intolerable that people should be knocked down and killed just when they are going to step off the pavement. The driver reiterated he did everything he could to avoid the accident. A juryman then accused him of not slowing down before he struck the victim. The driver agreed with this but stated he did not have time to slow down. The doctor who attended the accident was called and said the deceased died from internal bleeding and that all his ribs on one side had been crushed.

A cab driver who witnessed the accident was then called. He stated that the deceased stepped off the kerb just as the bus approached and thought there was no chance for him.

Mr Ellison said that Mr Winchester had worked as a driver for about eighteen months and that he had a good record with no previous accidents.

The jury returned a verdict of accidental death, which the coroner agreed with.

The first prosecution for the breach of the byelaws occurred in September. The case was brought, not only as a lesson to the defendant, but to the public in general. A Mr Frederick Gurr was bought before the court accused of smoking and using obscene language. He was asked repeatedly to put his cigarette out. He refused and became abusive. There were a number of ladies on the bus at the time. A passenger corroborated the inspector's evidence.

The defendant was fined £1 for smoking and 15s for the bad language. The chairman of the bench said the defendant's behaviour was disgraceful and that the breach of the byelaws was as bad as it was possible to commit.

In October's meeting of the Motor Omnibus Committee, the General Manager proposed a reduction in services for the winter months, but said that to run an efficient service next summer, he would need four extra buses. It was decided to order four more Milnes-Daimler double-deck buses, one of which would be a replacement for the Maudslay that was not delivered on time and subsequently cancelled. This would increase the fleet to twelve. Eight would be needed for the town service, two for the parade service, one would be being maintained and one would be available in case of breakdown. Four of the committee, together with the Transport Manager, were given permission to visit the Motor Show at Olympia.

The committee were in favour of this, except for Cllr Climpson who stated that buses were like policemen – you could never find one when you wanted one – and still advocated that Eastbourne would soon be having trams and that the fewer buses they had to sell for old iron when the trams arrived, the better.

It was also decided to convert the original single-deck buses to double-deckers with bodies built at the depot. The cost of the conversion was to be spread over two years. The four original bodies were sold for £30.

The General Manager informed the committee that the drivers were not being as economical with fuel as they could be. To combat this he had issued instructions for the drivers to turn off their engines at all termini and was only supplying drivers with enough fuel to cover their needs, but would be paying them a bonus on all unused fuel.

In December, a conductor was assaulted. Two men boarded on the way to the Archery. One man paid his fare, but the other refused. His mate gave him some money to pay, but he was reluctant to part with that also. Finally he paid, but then complained he had been overcharged, saying his fare should be ½d not 1d. The conductor explained the minimum fare was 1d. At the terminus he refused to leave the bus, so, as the bus needed urgent repairs, they started returning to the depot with the defendant on board. While on this journey, he struck the conductor on the right cheek, causing his hat to fly out into the road.

In court he denied everything, but the Chief Constable said this was his fourteenth appearance in court. The chairman described his behaviour as outrageous and added that a fine would be useless and sentenced him to fourteen days in prison.

The depot was expanded during the year to cope with the increased fleet. The extension was approximately half the size of the original buildings and cost £994. At this time Churchdale Road was known as Corporation Road.

1907

At the first council meeting of 1907, the members who had visited the Motor Show at Olympia reported back. They said they had inspected Milnes-Daimlers, De Dions and Thorneycrofts and recommended the purchase of four De Dion double-deckers at a price of £868 each. They could all be delivered by March.

At that time they had eight double-deckers, four of a fairly late type, but four somewhat older. One was presently under repair, but the other seven were operating all day and everyday to keep the winter service running. The four single-deckers were being converted to 'observation cars' and were not available.

During 1907 the number of complaints had dwindled but Col Cardwell was made of stern stuff and not for giving in easily and penned yet another letter complaining about the intolerable noise of buses running past his house in Upperton Road, asking for the service to be reduced. Again his complaint fell on deaf ears.

The Bus Committee reported to the council that the buses had made a loss of £252 in the last year. This compared to a loss of £318 in the previous year. The cost of a new storeroom, £178, had to be added to this making a total of over £700. There was no explanation as to how these losses could be reversed.

Mr Ellison, the General Manager, applied for a pay rise and was awarded a further £25 per annum. He also asked that engineering classes be given at the depot. He was given permission to do this. This was to be part of the Higher Education programme and a charge of 10s per lesson was to be charged. Mr Ellison was to be the teacher.

1908

1908 started with a deputation of residents from the Carew Road area of the town being allowed to address the full council to complain about their bus service, which was very sporadic with

The 1907 De Dion-Bouton with the crew in their new uniforms. (Eastbourne Buses Ltd)

One page from a 1907 wage book. Note the long daily hours and the hourly rate. It was normal for drivers to work 12- or 13-hour days. Apprentices were working for under 3*d* per hour. (Eastbourne Buses Ltd)

only four journeys per day in either direction, to and from the town. They commented that the area was a fast-expanding district of the town and that the limited service had been profitable. They added that the council's bus service had done away with Chapman's horse bus service, which, although not perfect, was regular and reliable. In true council style, they failed to make a decision, but passed it back to the Motor Bus Committee to discuss. The committee, having discussed this, proposed to give Carew Road a half-hourly service between 9.45a.m. and 5p.m.

This was referred back to the full council at February's meeting where it met further criticism. One councillor thought that a half-hourly service would never be profitable, whereas another councillor thought it amusing that the Bus Committee must think residents of that area must go to bed at 5 in the evening and thought the service should run until later in the evenings. Another councillor thought the fare of 1*d* was excessive and people would be reluctant to pay this. One councillor said that he had seen one of the old, disreputable-looking observation cars in the area, adding that they looked disgraceful and should never be seen on the streets of Eastbourne again. It was then stated the observation car had nothing to do with the Carew Road service but was being used to take footballers to Hampden Park. (Was this the country's first football special?)

A councillor for the east end then asked why the residents of that area were not given the same consideration. They had been trying for a service for years. He was told that this would be reconsidered again in March. Finally they decided that they would agree to the Bus Committee's recommendations and the Carew Road residents could have their bus service. I use this as an example, but similar debates for services around the town were commonplace.

In March, an advertisement appeared in the local paper asking for tenders for the letting of advertising rights on twelve motor omnibuses. The contractor would be required to supply and fix his adverts to the ceilings of the buses, there being room for sixteen adverts on each vehicle. The winning bidder would have the rights for three years.

The question of the disposal of the observation cars arose again. The Chairman of the Committee thought they might be suitable for some towns but not for Eastbourne and that would clear the way for some electro-buses. The Borough Surveyor had been looking into the feasibility of converting them to dustcarts or water-carts and objections were raised that they should not be sold until he had reached a conclusion. Other councillors thought that if they were converted, they would still have noisy and smelly vehicles on the streets of Eastbourne. Another councillor said he had spoken to the Surveyor recently and he had decided that new vehicles, rather than converted ones, would be better. With this in mind, the Transport Manager was told to enquire how much he could get for the vehicles and report back.

A resolution was put that a delegation was sent to London to assess a new electro-bus, but a councillor was against this, saying that a bus should be sent to Eastbourne for trial. These buses would be virtually silent and emit no smells and therefore silence all the complaints from the residents. They were given the authority to buy four if they could arrange satisfactory terms for the sale of the four single-deck observation buses and hire of the batteries. Power to recharge these batteries would be purchased from the Corporation's own Electric Light Works.

The service had been expanding since its inception and the growth figures were as follows:

Year	Number of Buses	Number of Passengers	Profit (in pounds)
1903	4	430,722	2,384
1904	8	1,052,624	6,005
1905	10	1,328,723	8,039
1906	12	1,759,923	9,965

Cllr Hillman, who had supplied the above figures, made a long speech about the amount of complaints the committee had dealt with – in fact he could not remember a single meeting when at least one complaint had not been heard from a resident – saying that they should find a means of alleviating these complaints. He believed the electro-bus could be the answer, after having travelled on one in London, and stated he thought that all the claims made for it were perfectly justified. He went on to say that he knew there would be some opposition to it as the science was in its infancy, and they should await any improvements that were made, as there was no finality to the genius of man, but they should rid the town of the noisy, smelly buses as soon as possible. Converting to electric would increase the town's capital expenditure from about £12,000 to £16,000, but would be one of the finest speculations the council had ever entered into, resulting in a silent bus. To hoots of laughter he went on to say that he thought that one day we would all be flying!

By July, the Electric Vehicle Co. Ltd had written to the council giving a price for four of their electric double-deck buses and offering a price for the four observation cars. This offer, though, was rejected. The company also offered to buy and run the entire bus operation in Eastbourne. They were informed that they were at liberty to submit, without prejudice, any proposals they wished to make as to the purchase of the existing motor omnibus undertaking.

Cllr Hillman moved an amendment that they should purchase two electric buses. This, he thought, would be a more prudent measure, which he hoped would gain the committee's approval. He realised that electric traction had some drawbacks, not the least of which was that they were no good on inclines, so the buses could not be used on the Meads or Old Town routes. Unfortunately, although his amendment was seconded, it was defeated. It was hoped that the General Manager would be able to convert some of the existing fleet to electric operation. This conversion was never carried out – one of the reasons being the extra onboard equipment needed added 2 tons to the weight of the bus, which would increase vibration and make it more prone to skidding in wet weather. Running costs would be increased by 2*d* per mile (13*s* per day).

In October, the General Manager asked for authorisation to buy four second-hand De Dion-Boutons from a number of chassis on the market, as he would need more buses for the following summer's operation. He was given permission to do this with the approval of the chairman, subject to approval by the full council.

At the full council meeting, not all were in favour. When told that the chassis would cost £250 each and that bodies could be built at the depot for £50 each making a saving of £500 per bus, these costings were ridiculed.

Another councillor said that a bus was being converted to electric operation in Hove and that they should wait until the outcome of that experiment was known. Another detractor wanted to know why the chassis were on sale – there must be a reason for it. It was pointed out that the manager was a very experienced and able manager who knew what he was talking about and should be believed, rather than questioned so much. There was a small majority in favour of purchasing the second-hand chassis, so he got his way.

In December the council were asked to improve the livery from varnished wood to paint in a blue and yellow livery. The Liberals objected to this, as this colour scheme was Tory colours, and thought that the Liberal colours of pink and white would be better! Some councillors thought that it was not in keeping with the town to have buses in such gaudy colours and that the mahogany tint was far more fitting, but again the manager won the day and the famous blue and yellow livery began to be seen on the streets of Eastbourne.

1909

Buses dripping oil and petrol were still a problem and permission was asked to place sand bins at termini at a cost of £8 per bin. This simple solution was delayed by councillors who wanted to see how other towns handled the problem.

It was decided to help regular passengers by selling books containing fifteen 1d tickets for 1s. These proved to be very popular with nearly £1,000-worth being sold.

Mr Ellison, the manager, was a very clever chap. There was a problem with leaking radiators and the crews were using fire hydrants as a source of water to top them up, but Mr Ellison designed and built a new radiator at the depot for a cost of £11 each, as opposed to the cost of buying a new one for £25. This solved the problem and the committee authorised him to build seven more.

Coloured lights were fitted to the fronts of the buses to denote the route – blue for Ocklynge/Archery, yellow for Old Town and green for the Meads route.

The future of the noisy, unloved observation cars had not been resolved. The manager said he intended making one as quiet as possible for using as a relief bus on the Hampden Park route. He had also been in talks with the electrical engineer with a view to converting one for coal-carrying purposes and to carting coal for them at the rate at which they were currently paying. The electrical engineer was in favour of this and the manager was given instructions to prepare costings for this. When these suggestions reached the full council meeting, the suggestions were thrown out, saying that it would not be fair on the residents of the Hampden Park route to put up with such noise and vibration. (It really does make one wonder how bad they were.)

A passenger ended up in court for refusing to show his ticket. The defendant's solicitor stated that it had been intimated in some daily papers that passengers were not obliged to show their tickets. However, when one such case reached the High Court, it was decided that the byelaw was reasonable and valid. However the proceedings against Mr Lyons of Meads were dropped, although he was made to pay 2s 6d costs.

A painter from Seaside in the east end of town was not so fortunate when he appeared before the court for travelling without a ticket and using bad language. He had been the worse for drink when boarding the bus and admitted both offences, saying he would sign the pledge; nonetheless he was fined 5s on each charge.

Not all the 'Eastenders' were uneducated ruffians though. One, a Mr Brogdale, had a letter published in the local paper protesting about the complaints from a previous correspondent signed 'A Visitor'. The latter had penned a letter saying he had been staying adjacent to the Burlington Hotel on Grand Parade and had a conviction that the 'combined hideous noise emanating from buses, nigger minstrels and the Salvation Army are rapidly and effectively ruining the resort for visitors of the better classes'. He went on to make a disdainful reference to the multitude who lived in the back streets.

Mr Brogdale argued quite eloquently that the councillors were better equipped than 'A Visitor' to judge what was right for Eastbourne and their judgement was proving correct as the popularity of Eastbourne as a health resort and watering-place was increasing. He also brought into question the visitor's ability to differ between nuisance and entertainment and noted that the Salvation Army were much more than entertainment anyway. He finished by saying that as a working man, he took the reference to the back street multitude as an insult.

The visitor was not alone though. A deputation, consisting of many residents from the area between the pier and the Grand Hotel, met the council, including letters from ten medical men. Managers of three of the largest hotels, including the five-star Grand Hotel, tendered their apologies. They estimated that £4,000 was being lost by rooms remaining empty in hotels and houses along the front parades, due to the noise and vibration, and due to the buses catering for people who wanted rides on the cheap. They had heard that in Brighton electric buses were operating successfully along the promenade and in the best parts of the town and demanded to know why they could not be used in Eastbourne. They were in possession of the offer made the previous year by the Electric Motor Company.

Many councillors were sympathetic to their views and thought they should be listened to as they contributed greatly to the rates. On the other hand it was argued that 22,472 people had rides along the seafront in July alone and who were the owners of a few hotels to deny them this pleasure? A motion to stop the service in September was lost and the Mayor said that was the end of the matter and it would be relegated to the waste basket!

The camber at the road junction at the Lamb Inn, Old Town was still causing problems. The manager made a visit to the site with the Borough Surveyor but decided that no improvements could be made without considerable road widening and this would have to be deferred until a future meeting.

The manager had also been at work trying to make the De Dion buses quieter and produced drawings on modifications to the gearbox. One bus had already been fitted and he invited the committee to inspect the vehicle, as well as the depot, as he was unable to cope with the necessary rebuilding and repairs needed for next season with the limited space at his disposal. This meeting took place and the Borough Surveyor was asked to submit alternative plans for the alterations that were now needed.

By October no offers had been received for the observation cars and the manager was given permission to use one for carting and towing purposes, and to dismantle the other three with a view to reusing any parts possible.

When the Borough Surveyor presented his plans for the extension to the depot, he also submitted plans to build a new depot on land opposite the existing depot. This would be built on land owned by the Duke of Devonshire. The Duke's agent had agreed to the sale of the land, measuring 1,277 square yards, for a sum of £450. The cost of this new depot would be £4,070 including the price of the land. His plans were accepted and he was authorised to proceed with preparing detailed plans and specifications. It was envisaged that the new buildings would be used for storage whilst the workshops would remain at their present location.

The manager reported that more buses would be needed for the following season and to replace the worn-out ones and there was now an opportunity to purchase some at a low price. The committee was given authority to spend £1,800 on vehicles. They inspected nine De Dion buses owned by the Associated Omnibus Company and it was decided to purchase all nine. Three were purchased in 1909 for £900; the other six in 1910.

1910

Mr Ellison was awarded another pay rise of 25 per cent, raising his salary to £400.

The new part of the depot was built opposite the existing depot on the north-east side of Churchdale Road and was the start of what most people recognised as the depot that lasted to the 1970s. The extensions to the workshop included a blacksmith, and a copper and tin-smith's shop as well as a paint shop. Additions to the machine shop were also planned with a bigger, stronger electric motor to drive the lathes. Four other machines were also required and the manager suggested he purchase second-hand machines at a cost of about £160. These machines, it was claimed, would help with service reliability and noise reduction. His plans were approved.

Snobbery was still very much alive in 1910. The Motor Bus Committee had decided that advertisements should be allowed on the nine new buses, but Cllr Breach thought that this should not extend to the seafront routes. He thought it was a 'great nuisance' to have advertisements on the parade buses. The council had prosecuted people for doing the exact same thing as they were now proposing to do themselves. He thought that those people on holiday should not have their attention arrested by tradesmen's 'tombstones' and they should have as little nuisance as possible. Cllr Fear pointed out that they should have more interest in the advertiser's point of view. It was then pointed out to him that he was an interested party and should not be taking part in the debate! Other councillors pointed out that the council, by seeking parliamentary powers to restrict the liberty of tradespeople and especially to prevent large hoardings and advertisements being erected in the streets, were being very hypocritical. A vote was taken and a ban on advertising on parade buses was passed by a single vote.

Some councillors were still putting the wishes of the large hotel owners and upper classes before those of the smaller hoteliers, east end residents and financial viability of the company. They proposed the seafront service should be restricted to two buses, except for Bank Holidays when it could be increased to four. Luckily these councillors were in a minority and their proposal of a restricted service was outvoted by a large majority.

The Eastbourne Schoolmaster Association asked if they could be allowed to hire buses for school parties, but were told that an agreement had been reached with the cabmen that parties could only be taken on bus routes and the appropriate fare was to be charged, so their request was denied.

An article on Eastbourne's motorbuses appeared in an edition of the periodical *Motor Traction*. It opened by saying that Eastbourne was one of the few south coast resorts that had held aloof from tramways and there was little doubt that this policy would serve to maintain those distinctive features that render it peculiarly attractive to the better class of visitor. It continued that it would not necessarily be fair to say that trams and trippers went together, but seaside resorts that catered for the masses had tram systems, whereas Eastbourne and Folkestone, both towns which depended on the more moneyed class, had taken the opposite line.

They praised Mr Ellison by stating that, although the fleet of buses was not that modern, he had kept them reliable and profitable. He had increased the fleet threefold since he took over and had equipped the workshops and had plans for expansion. Details of the plans were given, including parking for twenty-five buses in one large building and, to the right of that, offices on two floors that would include an office for the manager, general office, public counter and storerooms.

From the financial side they pointed out that the buses had just had their best year making a net profit of £600, compared to £250 for 1908–9. They were of the opinion that this figure would have been more if the buses were not charged with running loss-making services during the winter months. (This situation only lasted for about the next century!)

The council were asked to allow the staff to have a bus for a staff outing. A councillor asked how it would be possible for all the staff to go on the same day. He was told that they planned to have a day out on a Sunday. Alderman Keay thought this was a confession to be ashamed of and that the council were practically acquiescing to the use of buses on a Sunday. He thought the problem could be overcome by having two outings on another day with half the staff going one day and the other half the next.

The Town Council had been successful in attracting the Royal Agricultural Show to the town and wanted special buses to take visitors to the show. The agreement with the cabmen arose again, but some councillors thought that there would be enough trade for everyone and it would not look good if after attracting the show and visitors to the town, they could not get to the show. It was decided on the narrowest of majorities to allow the special buses to run.

In September, another driver was taken to court for speeding. The offence took place from Langney Road into Seaside. PC Bean testified that the bus was being driven between 15–18mph and he watched it for about 100 yards and its speed did not slacken. Another officer, PC Standen, also witnessed the event saying the bus 'passed at a speed that was much too fast and it swerved in its path. It would have stood no earthly chance if a vehicle had come from a side street.' Another witness stated that the bus came past so suddenly and so fast that he could hardly stand still. It shook him all over and he had to go home to sit down.

Mr Mayo, defending, said he protested that the defendant was only given one day's notice of the trial, which was not long enough to find witnesses, but said he was not travelling at more than 12mph. Indeed it was an old bus and it would not go at more than 12mph. His conductor and an inspector backed this up. Another driver said he had driven the bus the previous day and he doubted that the bus was capable of more than 12mph and he had had a problem getting it to move up Ocklynge Hill.

Unfortunately for Driver Fred Bushell, the magistrate believed the prosecution and fined him 10s.

Mr Ellison had also invented and patented a new sort of emergency brake and the committee went to see this in action. The Motor Bus Committee recommended to the full council that the whole fleet be equipped with this new invention. It was also recommended that Mr Ellison be paid £15 for out-of-pocket expenses on the understanding that the Corporation be able to use his invention for all time.

1911

Following numerous complaints from residents in the Old Town area of Eastbourne about buses splashing their houses with mud as they passed, Mr Ellison, although denying that the buses were wholly responsible, tried experimenting with splashguards on the wheels. Although they were effective, they were very unsightly and Mr Ellison recommended they were not used as they could have posed a risk to the public and he could not countenance this.

Another of Mr Ellison's improvements was a screen for the drivers and these he could manufacture and fit for £1 each. Waterproof aprons were to be fitted to all the buses.

A bus was also to be decorated for the Coronation of King George V and Queen Mary using minimal national colours.

There was disruption to the fuel supply when the employees of the Anglo-American Petrol Company went on strike. Mr Ellison sent two lorries to London to bring back twenty-four barrels of petrol to keep the service running. Two lorry-loads were also brought back from Shoreham Harbour. The Electric Light Committee wanted to take over the petrol storeroom used by the buses, and were told they could do so if they built the buses a new store. This was agreed to.

Mr Ellison informed the committee that buses 8, 9 and 10 had become too noisy and should be withdrawn from service. He suggested that No.8 be converted to a lorry for use by the Borough Surveyor and a buyer be sought for buses 9 and 10. This was agreed to.

1912

A conductor accepted a cheap watch in lieu of money for a 1d fare. It was decided to keep this watch for twelve months and if it was not claimed, then it should be sold!

It was decided to buy two more Leyland buses at a total cost not to exceed £1,500. Leyland did have an electro-petrol bus on the market, which was proving to be quiet and reliable, but it was decided to opt for the standard petrol design as great strides had been made in noise reduction. Mr Ellison again put his skills to good use and designed improved bodies of these two buses. Leyland agreed to incorporate these improvements in their build for a cost of £185 per bus.

In July, a long discussion took place on whether the fares on the seafront should be increased from 2d to 3d for the journey from the Redoubt Fortress to the foot of Beachy Head. The increase was finally agreed to, but the following week a letter appeared in the local paper stating that this increase was illegal, as the Board of Trade had not sanctioned it. The writer also pointed out that if two tickets were purchased for the same overall trip but paid in two stages, breaking the journey at the Grand Hotel, both fares being 1d, the journey could still be done for 2d.

A Leyland bus before registration and delivery to Eastbourne. (Author's collection)

Another prolonged debate occurred over the siting of a bus stop at Hampden Park. Although Hampden Park is now a sprawling suburb of Eastbourne, at that time it was just a large park with a few large mansions bordering it. Two of the owners of these houses were complaining about the bus stop being outside their property. One of these was Alderman Martin, whose building firm was constructing more property there and who claimed he could not let these properties while the buses terminated there. Many councillors and the press thought that Mr Martin's views were being given too much consideration due to his position and finally a cartoon on the subject appeared in the local paper.

In June, there was a railway accident at the mouth of Eastbourne Station, when a steam locomotive was pushing some vans and four coaches back into platform 3 to form the 3.40p.m. train to Tunbridge Wells. The leading vehicle became derailed and dragged the vehicles behind it off the rails too. The brake van and bogie carriage overturned, causing considerable damage to the wooden vehicles. A steam breakdown crane had to be summoned from New Cross Gate, London. This duly arrived at 6.35p.m. The crews got to work and remarkably had the line cleared by 8p.m. All lines in and out of Eastbourne were blocked during this time and Mr Ellison had been telephoned to see if he could help and, according to the newspaper at the time, 'came to the rescue of the railway authorities in a way that surpassed all expectations'. He supplied eight buses, some of which were taken from the Old Town service, and a 5-minute service to Hampden Park Station was established. Hundreds of passengers were moved, including a party of seventy-four who were bound for Heathfield, and filled two buses. Twelve of the railway company's vans were used to transport passengers' luggage and the mail. Each of the eight buses supplied made two round trips every hour and managed to transport about 1,000 passengers every hour.

1913

A councillor asked if used ticket boxes could be fitted to the buses, but was told that these had been tried in the past but had not been successful.

Advertising on the buses was another controversial subject, with some councillors thinking that all contracts should be arranged 'in-house' rather than using an agent. It was finally agreed to employ the services of Messrs Griffiths and Millington who would pay £35 per bus.

A telegram had been received from Leyland guaranteeing delivery of six new buses before next Easter, the cost of which would be £745 each. The Motor Bus Committee recommended the purchase of these to the full council and after some consideration they agreed. The seating arrangement of the two Leylands already running, as well as the proposed new ones, was discussed as they were the first buses to have transverse seating rather than seats running down the sides of the vehicles. Some councillors preferred the original layout and were against changing.

By the end of the summer, passenger numbers and profits were down on previous years and twenty staff had to be laid off for the winter months.

Fuel consumption of the buses was improving with the later buses managing 9 miles per gallon, compared to 5 miles per gallon of earlier vehicles. This was due to better tanks that fuel did not evaporate from and new carburettors that the manager was able to adjust. These measures had led to a saving in fuel of over 1,600 gallons in six months.

Passengers were still not allowed to travel on the top deck between the Lamb Inn and the Tally Ho. On one trip, a passenger refused to come down, saying the conductor had no authority to make him do so. An argument took place and the bus was held up before the errant passenger, a Mr Baker, got off and walked. He was taken to court for breaching the byelaws. In court his solicitor stated that there was no byelaw to that effect. The prosecution agreed, but

NOTICE.

OLD TOWN ROUTE

Passengers are allowed to ride on top of the Motor Omnibuses between the Railway Station and the Lamb Inn Only, but (for the safety of the Passengers) not between the Lamb Inn and the Tally-Ho.

Tickets are issued to Passengers subject to their observance of this condition, which will be strictly enforced.

BY ORDER.

Original enamel sign telling passengers of the ban on travelling on the top deck between the Lamb Inn and the Tally Ho. Presumably this was on display at a bus stop in the Town Centre. (Eastbourne Buses Ltd)

stated that it was published under the terms and conditions of travel that no one can travel on the top deck between these two points and notices were displayed on the buses to that effect. His solicitor asked what would happen if the bus was full downstairs and there was no room for his client. The answer came back that he would have to stand inside. It was then pointed out that there was a byelaw stating that standing was not allowed inside and a regulation that standing was not allowed outside, but his client had a ticket and if he had to leave the bus then the Corporation would be in breach of their contract to take him to the Tally Ho. The Corporation said that this would rarely be the case.

When the defendant gave evidence, he stated that he had twice travelled up the hill on the top deck, and had also seen a top deck full of schoolchildren on a private hire and had taken this up as a matter of principle as he and many others found the regulation unnecessary and a source of inconvenience. He also knew of passengers who had to get off and walk due to lack of space on the bus.

Mr Ellison denied any knowledge of schoolchildren riding on the top, but another witness said that he was in charge of the children, confirmed it happened and had the tickets to prove it.

The magistrates retired to confer, but when they came back, they sided with the council and found Mr Baker guilty of wilful obstruction, fining him 1s with costs of £1 19s 6d.

Chapter 2

The War Years

Apprentices driving; Chapman's make history; shortage of staff due to war effort; severe overcrowding; buses for troops; employing clippies; gas-powered buses

1914

The conductors had had some near misses while reversing buses round corners at termini using red flags, especially at Ocklynge, which was on a main road. Cllr Pearson suggested a policeman be on permanent point duty at the site, but this was laughed at. The council decided to resolve the issue by issuing the conductors with larger flags!

At a full council meeting, Cllr Marshall asked why some conductors were only earning 4*d* per hour and working under 60 hours a week and questioned how a married man could live on these wages when rents were 10*s* or 12*s* a week. Cllr Niedermayer pointed out that their marital status was of no concern to the committee and that 4*d* was a training rate and fully trained conductors were earning 5*d*. It was also pointed out that buses were being driven by apprentices earning about 10*s* a week and although there was a saving to be made here, there was a greater risk of accidents occurring, with possible large compensation claims to pay.

Cllr Breach thought it was scandalous that apprentices were driving buses. It was pointed out that the younger members of staff must be put on to drive during part of the day, but were not allowed to drive during busy periods!

Cllr Huggett said he had seen boys driving on two occasions and would like the matter looked into very thoroughly. In the department's defence it was stated that Mr Ellison was very careful who he put in charge of a motorbus, and although they may be used in an emergency, they were still capable of driving a motorbus.

Mr Ellison commented on the statements made at the full council meeting about boys driving buses. He said that there were only two apprentices who were allowed to drive and these were twenty years old. He had personally tested them and thought they were capable and reliable and had no hesitation in awarding them certificates enabling them to drive any motor vehicle.

By February the De Dion buses were being rebuilt, with the bodies overhauled and repainted in readiness for the forthcoming season.

Charabancs were still operating tours from the seafront and the Watch Committee saw fit to refuse two applications for licences from men who lived outside the town on the grounds that those already issued were enough to meet the needs of the town.

Passengers were still not allowed on the top decks of buses travelling past the Lamb Inn up the hill towards the Tally Ho, due to the severe camber of the road. This prompted a letter in the paper from someone signing themselves 'Justice' which made the point that private parties, and even guests of the council in one case, were carried on top decks past the same point, and asked what the logic was behind this. He went on to point out that there were roads in the neighbouring towns of Brighton and Hastings that were infinitely more hilly and dangerous, but passengers regularly travelled on the top deck. Surely it was a matter of having efficient brakes and careful driving. There was much building work being done in that part of the town and something had to be done to cope with the increased traffic that would arise.

I suspect that this letter was written by Mr Baker who had been fined 1s the previous year for refusing to travel downstairs. He had not let the matter rest there and had appealed the decision to the King's Bench division of the High Court in the case Ellison v Baker. Unfortunately for Mr Baker it turned out to be a waste of time and money, because he lost again.

The six new Leylands were delivered and were found to be much quieter than the older buses, so it was decided that these should be used at night, as the noise made by the older buses was still a problem with the residents.

The council congratulated the committee on making a profit of £2,517 and thought that the current year should prove to be even better. One councillor made the point that £700 of this profit was for hiring their lorry to the Highways Department, and if they decided to invest in their own transport, this would have a large impact on the bus's profitability.

A Scotsman complained that the clock at Hampden Park showing the departure of the next bus was wrong and claimed for the cost of three lunches, 7s 6d, as he and his family were made to be late. The conductor admitted making the error, so it was decided to pay this claim. Some councillors were sceptical about this being a wise move, as they thought they had set a dangerous precedent and many residents would try to get a free lunch that way.

An unfortunate accident happened when a group of men from the Eastbourne Working Men's Club hired a privately owned charabanc for the day to go to Arundel. On the return journey three men thought it a good idea to sit on the top of the rear seat with their feet on the cushions. Whilst going round a bend one of the men lost his balance and fell backwards, taking two other passengers with him. All were found to be unconscious on the road. They were taken to Lewes Hospital where two recovered, but one unfortunately died. The coroner returned a verdict of accidental death.

The First World War started and this brought immense problems for the department. Seventeen staff had been called up for service and the question of their pay arose. It was decided that married men's wives would continue to be paid as if their husbands were still employed there. Single men's dependents would continue being paid as well, but single men without dependents would only receive half their pay. Territorials and St George's Cadets were given permission to travel free on the buses when on duty.

The army commandeered the batch of new buses, and the department was compensated for the money paid for them. The tyres were being hired from the Peter Union Tyre Company, a German firm, and the Town Clerk had been in touch with the Board of Trade to ask if payments to this company were still legal. The answer was that it was still legal but the tyre company was not able to send any of this money back to Germany and stringent measures were in place to prevent this.

By October the number of staff lost to the war effort was thirty-three.

The council were asked to agree to the purchase of six Leyland chassis and four complete buses, subject to the requirements of the War Office.

Chapman's, who were still operating charabancs, made motoring history when they organised a trip to Land's End and back. This week-long excursion was the first tour to include accommodation in the price of the trip. Twenty-two intrepid passengers made the trip in a Dennis vehicle. Many came from far away to take part, the furthest coming from Southport.

A group of bus drivers at the depot in 1914 before going off to war. (Beckett Newspapers Ltd)

Many were very impressed with the trip, so much so that they booked up for a forthcoming trip to Wales.

The new bus depot was a fine, purpose-built, red brick building with light grey coping stones. It incorporated workshops and body-building shops as well as a large bay for parking the fleet. That was in the days when skilled workers were appreciated and a road of sixteen semi-detached houses were built for them just around the corner. These houses still exist and the road is called Ecmod Road. Ecmod stands for Eastbourne Corporation Motor Omnibus Department.

About the same time on the other side of the road to the bus depot, the Eastbourne Corporation Electric Light Works was built in much the same style. Again three houses were built for their workers adjacent to the site. The electric works and the cottages have now all been demolished. In 1923 a railway spur was built from the main line mainly to supply coal for the Electric Light Co., but fuel and oil was also delivered to the bus garage by this means. Like many other branches and sidings throughout the country this met its demise in February 1967 and fuel was bought in by road.

1915

The war was beginning to take its toll; the department was running short of skilled mechanics as these were being taken by the Government for the war effort. A Government inspector had requested the department supply more skilled mechanics to help make ammunition. The manager informed this inspector that all mechanics of military age who were physically fit had already joined His Majesty's forces, but he would be willing to supervise the machine work and fitting in connection with the manufacture of shells using the machines at the depot if suitable machinists could be found to work them.

In May, a Private Rayne writing in the local paper said that after shooting two of the enemy at Ypres, Belgium, he was shot himself. The first part of his journey home was by train, and then he was transferred to an ambulance. He noticed that this ambulance was converted from a Chapman's motor-coach. There were two of them that were nicknamed the 'Eastbourne Canaries' due to their bright yellow livery and two canaries were painted on the windscreens.

An accident occurred when a bolt on the steering of bus No.24 broke. The bus collided with a horse and trap, doing some slight damage, and a Corporation scavenger was pushed down by his dust barrow and seriously injured.

In June it was decided that any servicemen in uniform would be allowed to travel for 1d. On Sunday afternoons one or two buses could also be used for driving out injured servicemen. Volunteer drivers would be used. Over one weekend in June, eight buses were used for these trips with the drivers only too pleased to volunteer their services. These buses left from the convalescent camp at the west end of town.

The committee was informed that the department's finances were in a healthy state and that a reserve of £8,000 existed to purchase twelve new buses when they became available. They would then have a fleet of twenty Leylands which they thought were the best available. A Leyland which had been in service for three years had just been stripped down and nothing wrong with its mechanics or bearings had been found.

An office at the Town Hall had been opened for men to volunteer to do munitions work at the depot, and several men had put their names forward.

Unbelievably a lady tried to claim compensation for her umbrella that was ruined when she had it raised whilst on the top deck and it came into contact with a tree. She claimed it was the driver's fault as he had driven too close to the kerb! Her claim was dismissed. She actually went to the trouble of appealing this decision. Her appeal was not upheld.

1916

There was good news from the War Department regarding the supply of new chassis to replace some of the buses that were long past their best. Leylands had been informed that they could supply Eastbourne Corporation up to ten chassis, providing this did not interfere with the needs of the War Department.

Due to the constraints of the war the evening services terminated about an hour earlier, except on Saturdays. Theatre buses were being affected.

Leyland reported that the new chassis that were due to be delivered would be stronger and more powerful than the ones previously supplied, but this would mean an increase in costs. The General Manager stated that he thought that the increases were entirely reasonable.

Sittings were held during the war to decide whether men could be excused military service due to their occupations. The Transport Department had lost many of their employees to the war effort. Six more drivers had been requested by the military, but Mr Ellison defended his position by saying he only had seven drivers left. The military representative said he didn't think that buses were essential to the town. Mr Ellison claimed one man was medically unfit for service. Three other men were given twelve-week stays and the other case was adjourned. These twelve-week stays were subsequently extended for another twelve weeks as Mr Ellison argued that the men were used to transport injured soldiers. Mr Ellison also argued that bus drivers in London were exempt. Asked whether he could not employ women drivers, Mr Ellison replied, 'If this course were taken, I would not like to be responsible for the safety of the public!'

A row erupted over the wages that were paid to the munitions workers. Mr Ellison was accused of paying his young female workers less than the £1 per week laid down by the Ministry of Munitions. Mr Ellison defended himself that only trainees were paid less, being 15s per week on starting raising to 17s 6d and then to £1 per week when fully trained.

From August, the department were told they could employ clippies. Cllr Breach said he hoped that these would be assigned to the new buses owing to the old buses breaking down whereupon conductors were expected to help the drivers to mend them and clippies could not be expected to do this.

A bus had been supplied free of charge on a Sunday to take the band from the military Summerdown Camp to the bandstand. Some councillors thought that as the band was paid for playing, they should pay for the bus. It was pointed out that the band members had all been injured fighting and they deserved free transport even though they had offered to pay for the hire of a bus. The free bus had been withdrawn about three weeks prior after operating for about six months. It was pointed out that the service had been started to give injured soldiers a trip out and to use this bus to take the band to a private engagement was an abuse of the privilege and playing for money may contravene the Sunday trading laws. It was agreed that the free service for the band would remain withdrawn.

The department was fined £1 for allowing a light to shine outside at night, which was against blackout regulations.

Demand for buses often exceeded supply and there was quite often a rush to board vehicles at the station. The department were denied permission to erect barriers to assist in crowd control and the police refused to supply a constable to assist, so the department had to employ an inspector between 11a.m and 9p.m. to control the numbers of intending passengers. This inspector received a rough time being continually abused, kicked, smacked in the face and once knocked over.

1917

By March, four new Leyland chassis had arrived; two had had bodies built and were in service and two more were having bodies built.

There was a call to reintroduce late night services as it was claimed that females were liable to being molested in certain parts of the town as they walked home. It was not possible to do this because of the continuing fuel shortages.

Ladies were continuing to make the news as one lady had applied for and been granted a licence to work as a taxi driver. An article in the local press reported this in the following article:

One swallow does not make a summer, and the general body of local taxicab drivers will probably be a little alarmed by the licensing of a lady applicant. There is no likelihood of any immediate overwhelming attempt to dethrone male occupants of the wheel, though further representatives of the fair sex will doubtless seek employment of this kind, as they are invading other fields of labour hitherto monopolised by the sterner portion of creation. Taxi driving has perhaps one incidental drawback calculated to deter women motorists. We refer to the liability to undertake the lifting of passenger's heavy luggage.

At a Military Tribunal in April, Mr Ellison again pleaded the case for one of his drivers to be exempt from war duties as he had a child and had recently lost his wife. Mr Ellison reiterated that he only had enough drivers to operate six buses. His application was refused but the driver was told he would not be called up before the end of May.

In May the petrol allotted to the buses was again cut by 20 per cent, leading to more cuts in services. This and other factors led to a drop in profits from nearly £4,000 to just under £700. Apart from not being able to run the mileage they wanted, the cost of fuel had risen to just over 2s per gallon from 1s 3d and there were problems in delivering the quantities allowed to the department.

It was reported that the girls who had been employed as conductresses were doing their work very satisfactorily. It was suggested that a seat be installed for the clippies, but this did not meet the approval of the committee. Unfortunately one of the conductors, Mr Charman, had been killed in action in France.

The De Dion buses were laying idle at the depot as work was being concentrated on newer vehicles, but it was hoped that these vehicles would be put back into service one day.

Private operators had got around the petrol shortages by converting their vehicles to gas. Nine such vehicles were operating in Eastbourne, each carrying a large gasbag on its roof. Most were used for pleasure trips into the country, but two coaches did a return trip to London twice every week. Chapman's were the pioneers of gasbags in Eastbourne and were operating well over 2,000 miles a week with never a vacant seat and could operate far more if they had the vehicles. Mr Chapman thought that this was not just a wartime makeshift arrangement but had potential for the future. Petrol costs on a round trip to London would cost £2 14s, whereas the cost of coal gas used would be under £1. On a trip from London to Eastbourne, a Chapman's charabanc had to stop on four occasions to fill the bag up, each refill taking about 13 minutes. There was an article in *The Motor* magazine in which the author was highly impressed with the efficiency of the new system and stated they were the most popular vehicles on the quiet Sussex lanes and went on to say that they were even competing with the railways on scheduled services.

Another local coach operator, Mr Bassett, thought there should be a network of garages across the country where the bags could be refilled using a meter system. A local garage owner, Mr Lovely, had indeed installed such a system on his premises and twenty-six car owners had already converted their cars to run on gas. Other potential customers from as far away as London had travelled to Eastbourne to view the system.

The poor inspector at the station was still getting knocked about and on one occasion was badly assaulted by a group of soldiers from the local barracks. The matter was taken up with Col Bostock but the matter could not be progressed as the soldiers had given false names.

In November, the Transport Department decided to look into the feasibility of using coal gas to power the buses. Mr Ellison was charged with converting as many buses as possible, but the committee were against having large gasbags on the roof. One councillor thought that gas cylinders would not be allowed but Mr Ellison had given the council the idea the buses could be converted using cylinders and was told he could do conversion using the 'necessary accessories'. However he was not allowed by the Board of Trade to put his ideas for converting buses into action even though the railways had been using a similar system for many years.

It was also reported that due to the poor lighting conditions inside the buses, some unscrupulous passengers were passing farthings off as sixpences. It was agreed to supply conductors with a small lamp.

1918

By January, Mr Ellison reported that he had received communication from the Home Office and His Majesty's Petroleum Executive that there were no regulations in force prohibiting the fitting of gas cylinders to buses and that he could go ahead with installing his system. A hitch in the fitting of compressors meant a short delay in the implementation of the system.

In March, the question of expanding the depot was discussed. Two plots of land adjoining the present depot in Churchdale Road were available for purchase from the Duke of Devonshire at a price equal to £1,600 per acre. The council were recommended by the committee to approve the purchase of this land. This recommendation was indeed approved.

By April, no gas-powered buses were running and Mr Ellison was coming in for serious criticism from councillors and public. Mr Ellison had said that some old bus chassis that were no longer used could be converted to dustcarts and water-carts. Many people thought that engineering skills should not be wasted on this when the country had more pressing needs of its engineers and that the old buses would be better used as scrap metal.

Chapman's had been refused a license for their services due to lack of fodder for their horses. However, they continued running their trips to Beachy Head and other places and due to this they finished up in the Magistrates Court. They had received a letter from the Ministry saying that horses fed on hay and roots were not fit for charabanc work. He was found guilty but only fined £1.

In August, the staff presented Mr Ellison with an illuminated address to show the esteem and appreciation of his generous action in recommending that a grant of £400 awarded to him for services in connection with the manufacture of munitions should be divided up amongst the employees. Mr Ellison had also recommended that a further £400 from the profits of the undertaking should also be shared amongst the staff. Councillors also spoke of their admiration for him for the way he had done his job and supported his staff. He replied that he was proud and happy in trying to do his duty with the Corporation.

On the August Bank Holiday Monday, only six buses were available for service and this was nowhere near enough to meet the demand.

In November, the General Manager finally managed to get a bus running on compressed gas and had a bus ready for inspection by the committee. The bus had been trialled and performed satisfactorily, bearing in mind the poor quality of the coal gas available. It was resolved at a committee meeting that the manager should get his invention protected by patent and the Corporation would pay the fee.

In November, Mr William Chapman died aged eighty-three at his home in Pevensey Road. Mr Chapman built and ran the first charabanc in Eastbourne and for twenty-five years ran horse-drawn buses. He owned the first motor charabanc in Eastbourne and was the first proprietor to run trips to Scotland and the West Country. He was also the first to run long distances with gas.

Thankfully the First World War had come to an end and the Transport Department could start planning for the future. In December the committee agreed to purchase ten new buses. Mr Ellison pointed out that the department only had eight buses operational. Three of these were using heavy war-subsidy chassis, while the other five had been in constant use since 1912 and were badly in need of a general overhaul. The Town Clerk was instructed to write to Leyland to ask if preference could be given for immediate delivery of ten new buses.

Chapter 3

The Post-First World War Years

New buses; homecoming celebrations; locally built bodies; Sunday services; General Strike; record-breaking takings

1919

The final figures of munitions made at the depot during the war amounted to 3,530 mines and 369,000 Stokes trench howitzer bombs, all of which had passed quality control and the workers were commended by HM Inspectorate for their efforts. A profit of £25,900 was made by the depot in manufacturing these weapons.

Mr Ellison reported to the committee that he had visited Leyland's factory and he had subsequently received a letter from them offering to supply four 30hp chassis suitable for double-deck bodies for £850 each and six long-frame 30hp chassis complete with a special type of enclosed saloon body with two compartments designed by Mr Ellison himself for the Old Town routes for £1,400 each. These buses had a capacity of thirty-three and had a saloon especially for smokers and if a lady sat in there, they would have to put up with the smoke as there should be room for them elsewhere. The Deputy Mayor presumed that ladies would not be permitted to smoke! These buses were designed this way as it was still not permitted to travel on the top deck up the hill from the Lamb Inn and these higher-capacity singles were seen as the answer to the problem. Another councillor asked what had become of the bodies removed from the chassis that were requisitioned for the war effort. He was told that these still existed and use would be made of them if needed. The four short chassis could be delivered by Easter and the rest by Whitsuntide. The committee agreed to the purchase of these.

A lively discussion took place at a council meeting as to whether the manager should be awarded a pay rise. An increase of £4 per week had been put forward, but one councillor thought that any increase for an employee already on £400 p.a. was out of order when a rise for very poorly paid road sweepers had just been turned down. It was also pointed out that there were still only six buses running on the streets of Eastbourne and this rise was not warranted. This was combated by the argument that he would have to do a lot of work to bring the service back to an acceptable level, that the town was better off with Mr Ellison and that he could earn much more elsewhere. In the true tradition of procrastination, the full council referred the matter back to the Bus Committee for further discussion! The following month, after more discussion, in which it was pointed out that he had taken over the undertaking when it was making a loss, had made a profit in each of the last twelve years amounting to £14,000, had contributed from the profits to the rate fund and therefore saved the residents money, Mr Ellison was awarded his pay rise.

In July, an angry resident wrote to the paper complaining that licenses to run charabancs on Sundays had been awarded. This went against all previous decisions that 'His Day' was being desecrated and would lead to a 'Continental Sunday' rather than our much-valued 'English Sunday'. A petition was presented to the council stating that after the stress and strain of the war years there was a need for a day of rest and quietness and requested that the licenses be revoked, but this was not successful.

1920

As a welcome home to the staff that had been serving in the war and as a general New Year's Eve celebration, part of the depot was converted into a theatre including stage, footlights, orchestra pit and curtains. The children of the staff were entertained in the afternoon, whilst in the evening the adults celebrated into the early hours. The children were treated to a tea, a ventriloquist and two films supplied by local cinemas. In the evening there were various solo performances from violinists, pianists and singers before the rest of the evening was given over to dancing, stopping at midnight to sing Auld Lang Syne.

Another attempt was made to make the carrying of dogs permissible, even if it was to be restricted to lapdogs sitting up the front with the driver. This attempt was again defeated just in case the dog interfered with the driver. Apparently ladies were not allowed to sit there either, for the same reason!

The crew pose alongside Leyland No.6, purchased in 1919. (Eastbourne Buses Ltd)

A line up of single- and double-deck buses in Gildredge Road in 1920, decked out for the carnival. (Eastbourne Buses Ltd)

Fuel was continuing to be a problem with another rise of 8*d* per gallon and the quality remaining very inferior. A letter was sent to the Board of Trade complaining of the above.

In April a visit was paid to the Leyland works to approve the design and inspect the quality of materials being used. The party were impressed with some double-deckers under construction for Birkenhead and Edinburgh Corporations and were assured the buses for Eastbourne would be equally as good, if not better. Delivery, they were assured, would start in May, ready for the Whitsuntide service.

Mr Ellison showed the committee a finished body he had designed and had built at the depot. They were very impressed with the end result and complimented him on the workmanship and finish of the body. By August the bus was in service and the general consensus was that it was an improvement on factory-built vehicles. In October, Mr Ellison requested that he be allowed to build five more of these bodies. He could build each one about £70 cheaper than Leyland could supply them at. These would replace seven very old buses that in his opinion should be scrapped. He was given permission to do this, and they were all completed by August the following year.

1921

The start of 1921 saw an investigation into how a profit of over £4,000, made during the summer, had completely disappeared by the end of 1920. Some of the loss had been due to the fact that the department had shown a sincere desire to re-employ the soldiers and sailors that had left to fight in the war. The frequency of service had not been reduced from the peak period when twenty-five buses were on the road and all staff kept on. It was agreed that the service should be cut and the staff agreed to cut their hours rather than have staff laid off.

In June Chapman's was formed into a limited company with a share value of £100,000, with 60,000 preference shares and 40,000 ordinary shares each of £1 each.

Even though the department had a record year for carrying passengers with nearly 6 million, a loss of £732 was still made. This was partly due to a sharp rise in the cost of petrol which saw the department's fuel bill rise from £9,446 in the year 1919–20 to nearly £16,000 the following year. The financial position was not helped by the fact they were still overstaffed as they continued to employ ex-servicemen. Some of these had been employed in levelling the land recently purchased to the side and rear of the depot. The benefit of this work would show up in future accounts. These men had also made 1,000 deckchairs for the Pleasure Grounds Committee.

In July the manager praised his staff for their professionalism, stating that there had not been an accident of any description during the entire year.

Mr Chapman (junior) was interviewed for the *Daily Mail* in July. In the interview he stated he was totally against pneumatic tyres for larger vehicles. He said he would rather have solid tyres with good springs rather than pneumatic tyres, whose walls had to be so thick they were virtually solid anyway.

On another subject he said that many soldiers had returned from the war and bought second-hand charabancs and although they were making a living during the summer, he was fearful that they would struggle during the winter. His own business was thriving, however, and a tour of Scotland he had advertised was so successful that instead of sending one charabanc, he was sending five, all fully booked. Each coach carried twenty passengers with a personal conductor at a cost of 24 guineas each.

To demonstrate how the perception of smoking has changed over the years, the following is a letter that was published in the local paper:

Sir,

Are you not just a little severe on the question of smoking in the buses?

I am one of hundreds of businessmen who daily use these vehicles and from the nature of my calling, am unable to enjoy the 'glorious weed' except between business hours. Rightly, the council have had a small portion of the bus set aside for those who enjoy 'My Lady Nicotine' and when you find as you nearly always do three-fourths of this compartment occupied by non-smokers, naturally you resent it.

Hundreds of times have I seen men get into the buses with a newly lighted cigar or cigarette compelled to throw it away because of the thoughtlessness of non-smokers. There is this to be said: To a stranger getting into our buses there is practically no evidence that the back compartment is a smoking one. This could easily be remedied by the pasting on each window of a placard 'Smoking' in a prominent place.

It is interesting to note that non-smokers had to go through the smoking compartment to reach their seats. At one time it was considered that conductors would have to ask non-smokers to leave the smoking compartment, but it was thought that that could lead to disputes and it was best to leave it to the etiquette of the passengers.

In October, Mr Ellison's wife died, while giving birth prematurely to a son. The baby boy survived. They had only been married since the previous January.

A much-restricted service was planned for the coming winter and it was envisaged that there would be a surplus of eleven conductors and eleven drivers. Again the staff were asked for their views and they agreed that the present staff should work shorter hours rather than lay staff off. They also agreed that the female members of staff should be replaced by male staff!

1922

Southdown opened a depot in Pevensey Road, Eastbourne, and operated a service from there using four buses. Both Daimlers and Leylands were used.

In June the Town Council discussed whether bands, bathing and buses should be introduced on a Sunday. A petition signed by over 2,000 residents was presented expressing thankful appreciation of the present quiet Sunday and the earnest hope it would be maintained. Others maintained that a poll of residents should be held to find out the views of the majority. Some councillors thought that financing such a poll would be illegal. One witty councillor said if the borough was sued, they could raise the money to pay the fine by holding a couple of dances at the bandstand! After over 4 hours of heated debate the full council decided to set up a committee to look into the matter.

This committee finally recommended that Sunday bathing be extended from 9a.m. until 11a.m. and to authorise band concerts in the Redoubt Gardens from 8.15p.m. until 10p.m. They thought the running of buses should be left to the Motor Bus Committee. It was decided to trial a Sunday service and run on one day only. This proved to be a great success with over 6,000 passengers being carried. This was all the more surprising, as the service did not start until 2p.m. The driver of the first bus was greeted by a large crowd and presented with a bunch of flowers. At the end of the day, Mr Ellison was there to see the last bus away, but that left with a full load and enough intending passengers to fill another two. Mr Ellison was subjected to much abuse from the throng. It was agreed by all that the trial was successful and this led to a restricted Sunday service being started. When the Sunday service first started, the crews were told that only volunteers would be used, but with a regular service envisaged, the men's contracts would have to be changed.

Jack as a conductor in the 1920s ... and as an inspector in 1958. (J. Cooke)

Mr Ellison's salary was increased by £75 p.a. to cover the work that he did on a Sunday. Cllr Buckland, who seemed to be against anything to do with Mr Ellison's pay and conditions, tried to prevent this increase, but his amendment to that effect was voted down.

The undertaking made a profit rather than the loss it made in the previous year. It rose from a deficit of £702 to a profit of just over £6,000. Just to prove you cannot please all the councillors all of the time, Cllr Chatfield was astounded by the profit and thought it was a bigger crime to make so much profit rather than to make a loss. Following on from this criticism, some of the bus fares were reduced by ½d.

1923

A conductor by the name of John (Jack) Cooke was employed in 1923. He was a long-serving, loyal member of staff. In 1978 he wrote down his memoirs and I include them verbatim below:

It was by train that I travelled to Eastbourne. I remember one Saturday in March 1923 (fifty-five years ago) I left the Black Country in the Midlands to travel by train to Eastbourne. On the following Monday I started work as a conductor on the Eastbourne Corporation buses, the oldest municipal bus company in the country. Whereas other towns had trams, Eastbourne Buses started off and kept to buses only and boasts the first bus service in 1903.

When I first became a bus conductor, some of the buses were past their prime. Some did not have a windscreen but a short board and an apron which did not help much to keep the driver dry and warm. A driver's uniform in those days consisted of breeches (navy blue) leather leggings, overcoat with peaked cap with leather top.

The seat alongside the driver was long enough to accommodate 2 or 3 passengers. The tyres on the bus were solid and when they got worn they developed flat spots on them causing the bus to go bumpety-bump along the road. Eventually they had to go into the depot to be pared and made smooth to finish off their life.

The lighting on the bus was gas, there was one high up at the front of the bus each side and one each side at the back inside the bus. Alongside the driver was a well with water in it. On the floor was a generator containing carbide, which was replenished every day. When it became dusk, a tube that was connected to the lights inside the bus was also connected to the generator, which was placed in the well and the water was turned on and the light lit with a match. There were no headlights, only oil lamps. The brakes consisted of a handbrake, which was for parking but pretty useless for stopping the bus. It operated on the back wheels only. The footbrake that operated on the flywheel under the driver's seat required a fair amount of pressure to stop and on occasions (it once happened to me) the lining of the brake shoe would fall off – hence for (sic) as I said the handbrake was almost useless for stopping. The gearbox was three- or four-speed, the lever operated through an open gate with plenty of grease on it, there were selector springs inside the gate to keep the lever in the desired position, therefore when they became weak, the gear change could not be made until the driver had bent down and pushed the spring over with his finger, hence a dirty greasy finger.

The canopy over the rear platform of the double-deck buses was about 18in wide and on a very wet day and the bus was full inside, the conductor was often very wet through within half an hour and had to continue with the rest of the shift, usually 8 hours. On one route in particular, the Hampden Park route via Kings Drive, there were no streetlights. So you can imagine the driver having to grope his way along a very dark road on a very dark night as, as stated earlier, only oil lamps were fitted instead of headlights. The last 50 to one 100   of roads before Park Avenue which I understand belonged to the Chatsworth Estate was not made up with tarmac. It had a rough surface with a beach topping and with holes in the road. A man was employed by the estate who, armed with a shovel, used it to shovel the beach back into the holes as the buses and other traffic passed over it. This was not the only discomfort – it also raised a cloud of dust- thus the conductors finished the day covered in white dust, as did the conductors on the Whitley Road route before it was made up with tarmac.

I remember in my early days as a conductor, the buses used to be so slow on the Meads route climbing the hill, that in the winter I used to jump off and run up the hill behind to keep warm, but that route had its compensations, being the prettiest in the town by virtue of the tree-lined route, the trees on each side of the road being so big that in summer the over-hanging trees met at the top forming a tunnel.

One day I was driving along St Philip's Avenue when I suspected trouble with the driving shaft. I called the conductor and asked him to stand in the middle of the gangway and tell me if it tickled his feet when the bus was in motion. He looked at me a bit strange, but to his amazement he said, 'Yes it did' so I decided to run the bus into the depot. The foreman looked underneath the bus and said he could not see anything wrong. Telling me to take another bus, he got into the cab to move it but had only gone a yard when the whole prop shaft dropped to the floor.

The buses in those days were not so reliable and frequently broke down, so the Corporation introduced a scheme called a 'non-stop' which meant that if we had trouble – sometimes an accelerator came adrift – we would tie the accelerator with string or get the conductor to sit on the wing with the bonnet up and hold it or plug a leaky petrol pipe with chewing gum, etc. We did our best to complete the journey and get a replacement bus waiting or get to the depot. If we succeeded in completing our journey without missing any part, at the end of the week we were rewarded with our non-stop prize of 1s 6d for the week. Had it not been for this 1s 6d when we had trouble, we would have been tempted to stay where we were and have a rest. However much the conductors contributed to saving our 1s 6d, unfortunately he did not get a share, as it was the driver's perk.

When conducting a bus, once I had an occasion to reprimand a boy on the bus, I did not know he was part of a large family who were a bit on the rough side, the next thing I knew two or three of them were round threatening me and this went on every time they saw me.

Conductors were brought up to help the old people on and off the buses and it was a regular sight to see them lifting small children off. Of course, the steps were higher and the buses were more leisurely, and nowadays it seems to be all rush with journey times cut down.

In the summer the drivers and conductors were issued with long white coats to protect the uniform and, well-laundered, always looked smart.

I think the most difficult buses to drive were those with dog gears. These buses had to be synchronised exactly when changing gear otherwise if you caught the edge of the gear it would throw back and it was likely to break your arm.

I remember one of my drivers, Old Bill we called him, during our stop at the Railway Station I popped into the cake shop and bought some fancy cakes and gave Bill one. Later I asked him if he enjoyed it and he replied it was all right but he could not get the paper off the back! (It was a macaroon!)

In those days we did not have canteen facilities like they do today and most of the duties were continuous for 8 or 9 hours no break, neither did we have vacuum flasks at that time. So Bill's daughter used to bring out a bottle of hot tea and when we got to the terminus near a pub, he would hand the bottle to me and say, 'Here, you get on with this. I'm going to have a pint.'

In 1936 I was driving a one-man bus along the seafront – a fourteen-seater. It was a lovely day but trade was slow because residents and holidaymakers in the hotels were listening to the funeral of King George V on the radio. When it was over the seafront became alive and I was overwhelmed so I had to ring the depot for a larger bus.

One amusing incident happened in Terminus Road. Travelling in the opposite direction to me a bus was following a slow moving horse-drawn railway dray. I pulled over to allow the bus to pass the dray, imagine my amusement when the driver of the bus failed to clear the back of the dray and the amazement of the horse driver when the horse and cart were being pushed along.

One hair raising experience I had one summer day, I had a full load of passengers, standing too, on the route from the pier to Hampden Park, a very popular trip in the pre-war days. While travelling along Lewes Road and crossing Enys Road I was on top taking fares when the near side wheels left the road, the driver and I decided to send the bus in. At that time we had single-deck buses and all double-deck buses were open-top. When the bus in question was in the depot it was fitted with stronger springs and an entirely new body fitted with a covered top deck. This was the first double-deck covered top seen in Eastbourne. It proved very popular and carried about twice as many passengers as the other doubles, schoolchildren waited for it and it was almost continually full, making it hard work for the conductor.

The social club at the depot put on a play entitled 'A Busman's Dream'. This was performed at the Town Hall and the Pier Theatre and over £100 was raised for the local Ear, Nose and Throat Hospital and the Eye Hospital. Although E.C.M.O.D. stands for Eastbourne Corporation Motor Omnibus Department, at a dinner laid on for the cast, Mr Ellison said it could stand for 'Excellent Comic Men Off Duty'.

At a Bus Committee meeting it was suggested that the Sunday service should start at 10a.m. rather than 2p.m. This suggestion was thrown out, but when it came before the whole Town Council, they overturned this decision and decided the service during the months of August and September should start at 10.30a.m.

It was decided to sell off disused bus bodies at 30s each not including the plate glass.

In July the fleet visited Eastbourne and a notice was put up at the end of the pier saying that any rating in uniform could travel any distance for 1d. Four hundred and ninety-two sailors took advantage of the offer.

The department required five double-deck bodies, but there was a shortage of skilled men and the Labour Exchange said that no body-builders were unemployed in Eastbourne at that time.

1924

Mr Ellison issued a writ for libel against one of the councillors who claimed that he had sold some scrap metal which was the property of the Corporation and other allegations over the fuel figures. Mr Ellison won his case and the councillor withdrew all his allegations.

A booklet was issued to crews covering all their rules and regulations. It is surprisingly similar to the current rulebook, with a few exceptions. Today a driver is given 10 minutes to make sure their bus is fit for service, as opposed to 45 minutes in 1924. However in those days the driver had to check more items: that the fuel tank and radiators were full; steering gear and brakes had to be carefully examined; grease caps should be checked: and all working parts lubricated. Drivers also had to check that leads to the sparking plugs were attached; and the brake drums, driving dog bolts and all nuts on the change speed rods were tight. Carburettor holding-on nuts had to be examined to see that they were tight and care had to be taken that oil drip-trays were empty and subsequently no oil leaked onto the road.

If a bus were full and there were passengers waiting at a stop the conductor had to give two rings to inform the driver they were full, who would have to slow down and shout 'bus full' as he passed the stop. Dial clocks had to be altered to show the time of the next bus. Passengers had to be picked up at any point but only set down at recognised stops.

Crews had to maintain a regular service and were not allowed to get within 200 yards of the bus in front.

If parked on a hill the front wheels must be pointed in towards the kerb.

The engine had to be started by pulling the starting handle up and never by pushing it down.

If the brakes or steering became defective the driver could take the bus out of service and return it to the depot without loss of pay.

When passing churches on a Sunday or hospitals at night, vehicles had to be driven slowly and quietly to minimise any noise.

Conductors were told to inform drivers of vehicles following closely behind when the bus was about to stop. They were also told not to signal for the bus to start if a vehicle was about to pass the bus.

Finally if the bus was involved in an accident with a horse, the colour, markings and sex of the animal had to be noted.

In January the manager reported that visits were made to two body-builders, Messrs Ford and Ashby of London and Brush Electrical Co. Ltd. He could not recommend Ashby, as their stock of timber was not up to standard even though £395 per body was the lowest estimate.

Brush, however, had bodies in various stages and workmanship and materials were very good. The manager recommended that they build the bodies that were required. By June, Brush had the five bodies ready for inspection. They were fitted to the chassis by Vickers Ltd of Crayford.

A driver was given permission to borrow the company lorry to go to an FA Cup match at Brighton, but was stopped by the police as the lorry was only licensed to carry goods not passengers. He was fined £1. Mr Ellison asked his committee to refund the driver and pay his expenses.

There was some good news concerning the price of fuel. It had been reduced from 1s 3d per gallon to 11d per gallon.

The manager asked that two spare Leyland engines at £285 and two back axles at £125 be purchased. This would mean less time off the road for buses as the components could be swapped over and the bus put back into service while repairs are carried out on the faulty item. This request was approved.

1925

Over Easter, the buses were exceptionally busy, until the weather changed for the worse. The department managed to get thirty-three buses into service. The August Bank Holiday was even busier and the entire fleet of thirty-eight buses was pressed into service. Over 62,000 passengers were taken, 3,824 miles were run and £437 was taken in fares.

Pneumatic tyres were becoming more prevalent and prices were sought from leading suppliers.

The undertaking continued to grow with record mileage of 759,973 and passenger numbers of 9,603,789 being recorded. This led to its own problems because at times the service could not cope and one contributor to the local press likened trying to board a bus on the seafront to a rugby scrum. They proposed a system be introduced as in Paris whereby intending passengers were given a numbered ticket and the conductor called them aboard in order.

The manager in his annual report said that the thirty-eight buses that were now in operation were not enough to cope with demand at times. In November the manager told the Bus Committee that ten new buses were needed. Passenger numbers were increasing all the time: in October there had been an increase of 120,000 passengers and the fleet was ageing. Six buses were thirteen years old, three were nine years old, fourteen six years old, ten five years old and four virtually new. He said it was questionable whether it was wise to try to keep maintaining the older buses and keep them serviceable.

Again he said that there had been no accidents of note of any kind over the last twelve months, which was a testament to the skill and professionalism of the staff. His words were slightly premature, though, as a fatal accident occurred a few weeks later when a gentleman stepped off a moving bus. A verdict of accidental death was recorded and no blame could be attributed to the crew.

The Bus Committee proposed that the full council accept a tender for the extension for the depot. The full council thought that the committee was out of order, as they had no authority to ask for tenders.

1926

The plan to extend the bus depot was met with some opposition at a meeting of the full council. Some councillors thought that the estimate of £13,000 was too much but the proposal for an extension was passed.

By June all of the single-deckers had been delivered and were giving good service. Bus No. 3 had its body rebuilt and enlarged and the seats were covered with the same moquette as had been used on the last buses to be delivered.

This was the year of the General Strike and the crews at the depot joined in. On the first day of the strike no buses left the depot in the morning, but volunteers arrived during the course of the day and a skeleton service was run. Some privately operated coaches ran on the Old Town and Meads routes.

Southdown did not fare any better with only three of their twenty-two staff reporting for duty. Southdown's management put out notices advertising for staff and they claimed that a full service could have been running by 10a.m. – remember there was no need for a driving licence in those days. The volunteers had come from many quarters including ex-servicemen, traders and ladies. These volunteers were not taken on because Southdown management thought that many of their employees had been intimidated and they were giving their staff a chance to return to work. The following day the service was running again, but some strikers boarded a bus bound for Eastbourne from Brighton at Rottingdean and tried to disable the bus by disconnecting a wire. These men were chased off the bus, the wire reattached and the service continued.

Eastbourne Corporation could not decide what should become of the striking busmen. Should they have preference over jobs or should the men who volunteered their services be kept on? Eastbourne Council could not even decide which committee should make this decision. Apart from the full council and the Motor Bus Committee, there was also an Emergency Committee set up to deal with the situation. In the end, it was the latter committee who took the decision to allow the striking busmen to apply for their jobs back as the service returned to normal. A reduced service was being run as many other workers were on strike and not so many buses were needed. Until the men were reinstated, they were required to return their uniforms, cash bags, punches, etc. Nine men applied for their jobs back almost immediately and they were all reinstated.

Another record August Bank holiday occurred. Over the three days, 167,161 passengers were carried, 11,500 miles run and £1,145 taken in fares.

The service was unable to cope at busy times. Four routes used the same stop at the railway station and those who queued were often unable to board due to those pushing in. This prompted another letter in the local paper where 'Might versus Right' and 'Last come, first in' seemed to be the chief considerations of those roughs. The writer had seen an instance of this selfish behaviour even at terminus buildings and at a time when a queue had actually formed: 'The bus arrived and four or five cunning persons showed their low breeding by slipping through a narrow way between the bus and the kerb where the people were lined up. Fortunately a bystander called the conductor's attention to this detestable ruse, and the man in uniform barred their way.'

The manager stated that the department required a small van and suggested a Trojan van similar to the Electricity Committee's be purchased. This was agreed to.

In September, it was decided to start fitting pneumatic tyres and a decision had to be taken whether to buy them or hire them under a mileage contract. The latter was opted for.

At the end of the season, the subject of laying staff off was raised again. This year, though, it was decided to keep on any surplus staff to help with the building of the new workshops.

A new siding was being constructed from the main railway line at Eastbourne. This siding was built primarily to serve the gasworks, but a spur was taken off this to serve the electricity works opposite the bus depot. The undertaking was to take advantage of this to have their fuel delivered by rail tanker. Petrol being delivered by rail would mean a saving of ½d per gallon. The manager suggested that a new pipeline was built connecting the tanker with their 8,000-gallon storage tank. He said that this would be a very good time to do this as the road was being reconstructed.

It was decided to extend the Sunday service to the winter months with a service that started at 10a.m. using five buses.

1927

The new depot was ready by the start of the year and was opened by the Lord Mayor and Lady Mayoress of London. They were greeted at the railway station by a guard of honour made up of drivers and conductors in full, smart blue uniform with yellow piping, many wearing war medals, before being taken by bus for luncheon at the Grand Hotel. After lunch, they boarded the bus again to go to the new depot. The new depot consisted of a complete block of repair premises, comprising an erection and machine shop, paint shop, woodwork and upholstering shop, foundry, blacksmith, electrician's shop, testing shop, cleaning shop and two store rooms. There was also a six-roomed house for the foreman as well as a new toilet block. The Lady Mayoress formally opened the depot before the Chairman of the Committee drove the first bus into it. The Lord Mayor's party then visited another part of the depot where a children's party was being held. They were then taken to the Town Hall for afternoon tea before returning to London at 5.20p.m.

Bus No.6, registration number HC 1451, had been purchased in 1919, and although the chassis was still serviceable, the body was past repair. A new body, complete with a larger smoking compartment, had been designed and built at the depot. It was ready for service and inspected by the committee.

Permission was obtained to allow a cleaner who lost both legs and an eye in the war to be employed as a steward in the social club's snooker room as it was not possible for him to find work elsewhere. He was paid £1 per week.

The social club was also given permission to hold a dance in the workshops in aid of the local pensioners and the children's summer treat fund.

The finances were improved due to two cuts in the price of petrol. Being delivered by rail, the price had dropped to 7d per gallon.

A bus wash was installed. The manager had attended a demonstration of the BEN washing plant and reported back that the cost would be £160 but this would be beneficial, as it would lead to efficiency savings.

The first covered double-deck bus converted in the works at Churchdale Road. (Eastbourne Buses Ltd)

One councillor thought that, despite having a new depot, the manager should seek parking spaces for four buses at the other end of town, so they could start from there in the mornings to save running time. Nothing came of this suggestion.

Another councillor thought that an old bus body could be used as a bus shelter. Other councillors thought this would not befit a town such as Eastbourne, while another councillor thought that some people might actually mistake it for a bus!

The manager thought that single-deck buses were the way forward and proposed to re-body some old doubles into singles. Buses 33, 34 and 35 had been purchased in 1916 and were capable of having their chassis reconditioned and giving excellent service. He suggested that the workshops build new single-deck saloon bodies that could seat thirty-six passengers for use on the Old Town route, which would alleviate passengers having to come downstairs between the Lamb Inn and the Tally Ho.

A petrol war between combine and non-combine companies had broken out and this had reduced the price of petrol to 6*d* per gallon, but the war between these had ended and the manager warned of steep increases being imminent in the cost of fuel supplies.

The manager was given permission to take the workshop staff to the Motor Show at Olympia, using one of the buses as transport.

Spitting was taken more seriously in those days and one passenger was fined 5*s* with 10*s* costs for spitting on the floor of a bus.

A move was put forward by the council to introduce season tickets, but the manager was against this as he thought this would have an adverse effect on income.

It was agreed that ten new Leyland Lion long-wheelbase single-deck buses (50–59) be ordered.

1928

The covered-in double-decker continued to cause controversy in the town – mainly from the councillors. They wanted to know if it was paying for itself. The manager told them that the cost of conversion was just over £800 but it was carrying about 9 per cent more passengers than any other bus, but there were no plans to convert or buy any more.

The advent of pneumatic tyres meant a large reduction in noise made by the buses. It was not long before the residents of Eastbourne were calling for the conversion of all solid tyres to pneumatic.

An editorial in the *Eastbourne Chronicle* said that serving on the Bus Committee was one of the least rewarding posts for a councillor to hold with every decision being criticised by someone. Lately though, it went on, criticism had been less because the townsfolk had been enjoying the best service ever and breakdowns were virtually a thing of the past.

However, they too thought that it was time that the old doubles were taken off the road, as, although they were fine in their grandfathers' days, they were now ramshackle, very noisy and uncomfortable, making travelling in them a punishment rather than a pleasure.

Smoking was still a matter of controversy. Smokers were still annoyed that ladies who did not smoke were still taking up their compartment. One correspondent wrote with what he regarded would be a good solution to the problem. This would be to put up a notice in the smoking compartment that it was reserved for ladies over fifty! This would ensure that no lady would ever sit in there. At a subsequent council meeting it was decided that smoking would be allowed on the upper decks of buses as well.

Although this eased the confrontations between those that wished to smoke and those who didn't, the letters to the papers carried on coming. A gentleman who signed himself 'A mere man' wrote that he thought that conductors should remove any ladies from the smoking compartment and continued 'nowadays many "ladies" have very bad manners. They are usually of the useless and certainly not ornamental type, and, in my opinion, men should always take the opportunity of politely snubbing them'.

Dogs were also allowed to travel on buses for the first time at the conductor's discretion. One councillor thought that dogs could be carried in a special trailer on the backs of buses but this idea was greeted by hoots of laughter and got no further.

A company called Greyline Parlour Coaches started a daily service to London. Advertised as 'the last word in safety and comfort', it had fares of 7s single or 8s 6d return. Seats had to be booked in advance but passengers could board at a number of points on the route.

The manager reported the price of petrol had risen by 4d per gallon. He also stated that the fleet consisted of fifty-six buses and that buses 9, 10, 11, 12, 31 and 32 had been scrapped. Some of the bodies were good and could be fitted to other chassis but he recommended selling them complete. If no sale could be made, he suggested they be dismantled and used for spares. Twenty-five buses still had solid tyres, but these could be converted at a cost of £65 per bus making a total of £1,625, plus workshop labour costs, but this would be done over a period of time. Mudguards would have to be fitted with the pneumatic tyres costing a further £7 each. Costs had been increasing and to break even they needed to carry twelve passengers for every mile, but they were only managing to carry ten.

In the years towards the end of the twenties and start of the thirties, a fund was set up by a Revd E. Browne of St Andrews, Meads at Christmas as an act of appreciation for the work and good service and manners shown by the bus crews during the course of the year.

In November a Leyland Titan covered double-decker was in town available for inspection.

1929

Sick pay was not a right and staff not fit for work were at the mercy of the Motor Committee for compassionate allowances. These were normally forthcoming. The Medical Officer of Health reported two conductors' families had infectious diseases and should remain away from work as a precautionary measure. The same compassion was shown to them and they received eight days' wages.

An apprentice called J. Moon was reported to have started in the upholstery shop. And he was still there in 1972 when I started!

A one-man-operated bus produced by Dennis Bros Ltd was shown to the Board.

Times were not good and a loss of £507 for April was presented to the Board, even though an extra 13,000 passengers were carried and over 6,000 more miles run. The increase in petrol alone came to £420. The cost of buying pneumatic tyres could not be reduced so they were hired at a fixed rate of 0.624d per mile.

The Bus Committee had expressed themselves in favour of closed-in double-deckers, but the Deputy Mayor took a different view. She thought that they were unsuitable because the roads were not wide enough and felt bulky vehicles would spoil the look of the streets. The Chairman of the Bus Committee retorted that many workers had to go to work in the rain and didn't have time to wait until there was space on a single-decker, so were forced to sit upstairs in the rain. The committee therefore stuck to their recommendation that six covered doubles be put into service. One councillor reminded Mr Ellison that it was not so long ago that he was stating that single-deckers were ideal for the town. It was eventually decided to invite tenders for six double-deckers with roofs.

The talents of the busmen were on show again at the town's Hippodrome Theatre where a play called *The Inca Love Call*, written by a bus driver, was being performed and receiving good reviews.

Profits of the concern were down again, but this was put down to the high level of service given which was not enjoyed by many towns, the increased cost of fuel and the fitting of pneumatic tyres.

A small fire broke out in a coach that was parked on a piece of waste ground. A passing policeman spotted this. A policeman and an ice cream man extinguished the fire with some water supplied by the ice cream man after trying to stamp it out failed. The story made the national press the following day, but by then had been exaggerated that the policeman used ice cream to extinguish the flames.

A visitor managed to put his head through the side window of a bus. He had just boarded in the town centre and to make sure he was on the right bus, he went to ask the conductor who was standing on the pavement. Unfortunately the window that he thought was open wasn't and he put his head clean through it. Luckily he was wearing a soft hat, which saved him from serious injury.

The buses had again broken all records for 1928 when the accounts were published in August. They showed more passengers were carried, more miles were run and more revenue taken than ever before, but due to increased costs, profits dipped.

At the end of the season, the question of laying off seasonal staff rose again. The manager suggested that in order to retain all his staff, they should all have a day off and only work six days a week instead of seven, having every second Sunday off. This would mean drivers receiving a weekly wage of £3 10s a week.

In September the three one-man Dennis buses were delivered at a cost of £1,845.

The manager still thought that enclosed single-deckers were best carrying up to forty passengers; however the Heavy Motor Car (Amendment) Order of August 1927 made it impossible to increase the carrying capacity from thirty-two to forty owing to the dimensions of a bus being fixed. Therefore to deal with peak traffic, double-deckers were required. There had been opposition from the council towards closed-in double-deckers, but the manager needed the full backing of the council before any new buses could be ordered, so he arranged for a new closed-in double-decker to be in service in Eastbourne between 19 and 22 December so council and public could approve or otherwise.

Chapter 4

The 1930s

Covered double-deckers; the fight to run to the top of Beachy Head; Traffic Commissioners; smoking – a burning issue; updating the fleet; record expansion

1930

Councillors were invited to take a ride on the first closed-in double on a very wet morning. The following amusing article appeared in the local press:

Councillor Avard detached himself from the group at the Town Hall. All of us watched with bated breath. There he goes! By gum! I believe he is going up top! He is! Great Scot! There he is up top! With one accord we were all agreed that it would not be safe with such a weighty councillor on the top deck, but nothing would shift Avard. Two or three councillors bravely went up top to try to smoke him out, but even some of the councillors' pipes have not got that Havana touch. Avard had sat down; it was enough. Strangely also by degrees we had all got up to the top deck. The rain ripped, the wind tried to beat the previous week's gales and all had got the danger-laugh – the jokes so readily flying about when Britishers are in peril. Up the steps came the chirrupy Manager with a face wreathed in his usual smiles.

'Please watch me. The old top-decker will pull up alongside and I will take a seat on the top and you will then see, ladies and gentlemen, that both the buses are the same height.'

A few of us did notice the gentleman taking his bath in the bathroom on the top of the other bus after he had knocked frantically at the window to draw attention, but most of the Bus Committee were so busy showing each other the latest improvements that the poor Manager was quite forgotten and was last seen being rescued by a type of life-buoy. In the meantime the Chairman of the Bus Committee was so proud of a new-fangled exit ladder in case of emergency, that nothing would tear him away from it. The whole of a Scotch dictionary was used in explaining it.

What a frightful argument there was in deciding which would be the best roads to drive along, and how some of the faces blanched when Granville Road hill was suggested, and how happy everyone was when the Manager suggested 'just round somewhere and back again'. The somewhere was not quite level ground and the distance was not quite half a mile.

What a strange sight it must have been for the natives. Certainly we did observe many open-mouthed stares at the appearance of a top-decker with no passengers on the lower deck. Some of the natives must have thought that the occupants had all gone upstairs to sleep.

At a subsequent council meeting, some councillors argued that doubles would make financial sense and ease traffic congestion, whilst others questioned their safety on all but the flattest route. Finally, it was decided to go ahead and purchase twelve double-deckers. One councillor hoped that these vehicles would not be disfigured by unsightly adverts. Other councillors agreed.

The first of these Leyland Titans went into service on 1 July 1930.

Smoking on the buses was still a problem. It was reported that sometimes a non-smoker or lady was sitting in the smoking compartment taking up the room of a smoker, so it was moved that smoking be allowed in all parts of the bus and ashtrays fitted accordingly.

The proposal to run a bus service to the top of Beachy Head was called outrageous by one angry contributor to the local paper. He said that the Downs had been purchased by the council in order to preserve the beauty of the neighbourhood. He found it unbelievable that those very people who set out to preserve them planned a bus service, asserting it was:

Already a hideous spectacle every Sunday with hundreds of motors dashing along making screeching noises, and sending up clouds of dust for hundreds of yards. Great char-a-bancs grind along bearing loads of people who would much prefer to remain on the beach and who care nothing for the stretch of downland with its glorious views of sea and countryside. Is the Town Council to add to this horror?

Another contributor wanted to know how they could continue to advertise the tranquillity of the Downs if they allowed the noisiest of traffic to run over them.

An accident occurred between a Southdown bus and a Rolls-Royce in Ocklynge in October. The bus was coming down the hill, when the Rolls-Royce pulled out of a side turning on the right and collided with the offside of the bus. Despite witnesses stating that the driver of the Rolls was travelling too fast and crossed to the wrong side of the road as he turned, the driver of the car said that at the moment of impact he was stationary. The Mayor, who heard the case, said that there seemed to be a general impression that the user of a main road had a greater right to the road than one coming out of a side road. That idea was erroneous. The bench thought that it was not safe to convict and dismissed the case!

A Leyland single-decker. Note that not only does this bus carry the town's crest but also the words County Borough of Eastbourne. (Eastbourne Buses Ltd)

One of three Dennis single-deckers delivered in 1929. (Author's collection)

The Road Traffic Act 1930 brought major changes throughout the motoring industry. Driving licences were introduced and age limits were imposed on certain classes of vehicle. This had far-reaching effects on the bus industry with a whole section of the Act concerning buses. The licensing of bus routes was taken away from the Board of Trade and given to Traffic Commissioners. These commissioners served different areas of the country and there were three commissioners to each area. The Minister of Transport appointed these commissioners.

Public and private undertakings had to submit their plans for services to them and they decided on whether a proposed route met with their approval depending amongst other things on the suitability of the route, the extent to which the route was already served, whether the proposed service was necessary or desirable and the needs of the area as a whole.

The commissioners also had the power to force operators to submit to them the types of vehicles to be used on routes, a copy of their timetable and fare table. They also had the power to fix the fares to be charged.

The Act also forced operators to hold a Public Service Vehicle licence. These could be refused or revoked if the holder appeared not to be a fit person to hold such a licence. The vehicles also had to be maintained to a certain standard and a Certificate of Fitness had to be issued before it could be used on any service. Any alterations to the interior also had to be passed as being fit for use. Each certificate lasted for five years before renewal. Certifying officers appointed by the commissioners carried out these checks, and they also had the powers to enter, stop and inspect any bus at any time.

Not only did the owners and vehicles have to be licensed, but so did the drivers and conductors. Minimum age limits of twenty-one for drivers and eighteen for conductors were laid down, although if they were already employed as such and could prove it, they could carry on working. These licences could be revoked on the grounds of conduct or disability.

The Act also laid down new speed limits. For cars fitted with pneumatics tyre there was no limit, but for every other class, limits were laid down. Buses were restricted to a maximum of 30mph.

1931

Until 1931 anyone wishing to reach to the top of Beachy Head had to travel by an excursion coach, as no stage carriage service existed. Before the Road Traffic Act 1930, the Watch Committee had granted licences to private firms to run trips to the top of Beachy Head, but all proprietors agreed not to pick up or set down passengers on any Eastbourne Corporation bus route.

On 22 June 1931 the Traffic Commissioners wrote to Eastbourne Corporation, Southdown Motor Company, Chapman & Sons, Southern Glideways Ltd and the Eastbourne Motor Coach Association stating that there was a need for a stage carriage service. Excursions licences forbade the sale of single tickets and they thought there was a public need for the latter. They felt this was a matter of urgency and that applications to run this service should be submitted no later than 29 June. The relevant application form was included with the letters.

Eastbourne Corporation duly completed the forms and they received confirmation from the Traffic Commissioners that they had been received. Mr Ellison then went on holiday to Scotland where he stayed at the Great Central Hotel in Glasgow.

Meanwhile Southdown made applications for licences to run a temporary service. Whilst in Glasgow Mr Ellison saw an article in the *Evening News* saying that a temporary licence had been granted to Southdown. This licence covered three weeks in July. Mr Ellison was surprised at this because the Corporation was unaware that the licence application had been considered and had had no opportunity to make representations, so he telephoned the Chairman of the Commissioners, who told him that he thought that the Corporation did not want the business because they had not filled in form 49. He replied that he had filled in the form that was sent to the department by the commissioners (PSV8). The commissioner appeared not to wish to discuss the matter further and hung up.

When Mr Ellison returned to Eastbourne he advised the Town Clerk that there was no appeals procedure to the commissioners, but an appeal could be made as an aggrieved party to the Minister of Transport.

Eastbourne Corporation was, however, granted a temporary licence for the same period and was allowed to run a 30-minute service in conjunction with Southdown.

Southdown issued special bills advertising their new service and had made large boards saying 'Top of Beachy Head' and attached them to the sides of their buses. Southdown then sent in a formal objection to the Traffic Commissioners to the application by Eastbourne Corporation to run to the top of Beachy Head on the grounds that they were running a satisfactory service.

On 8 July Mr Ellison replied to a letter from Southdown inviting him to a meeting at their Pevensey Road depot, stating he could not attend without the consent of the Transport Committee. Representatives of other companies attended and it was resolved at this meeting that 'the operators of Motor Coaches are unanimously of the opinion that a stage carriage service to Beachy Head is not necessary, and the needs of the public can be met by a service of Express Carriages charging 1s single and 1s 6d return fares, running as traffic demands and not to a fixed timetable.' They stated that if the commissioners accepted this resolution then all the previous excursion licence holders would continue to share in the traffic and that the Stage Carriage licence applications would be withdrawn.

The Traffic Commissioners met between 6–8 August to decide who should run the service to the top of Beachy Head. Their report covers 289 pages. Eastbourne Corporation did not get off to a good start as the commissioner pointed out that in a report from them they proposed that the situation should not alter whereby the stage carriage service along the promenade and excursions to the top of Beachy Head run by all the companies should continue. The Corporation also stated that they did not think it proper to run a route along the seafront to

Leyland PD2, fleet No.79, before it was converted to an open-topper. Note the starting handle. (Robin Bennett)

the top and they should not undertake the responsibility for this service. The commissioner thought it extraordinary that now, only a few weeks later, they had now come forward with a substantive application that excluded all other operators.

The commissioners were of the opinion that the smaller applicants were not in a position to be able to run a good regular service and that their vehicles were only licensed for express carriages and would not fulfil the criteria to be licensed for stage carriage.

The chairman also questioned witnesses as to whether they thought that if rival companies competed on this route, it could lead to drivers racing each other. There was also the question of the nature of the road to the top, Upper Dukes Drive, which contains a few hairpin bends and whether two buses going in opposing directions could pass on these. It was suggested that vehicles coming back down should take a different route, the Beachy Head Road and Chesterfield Road. There is still an unwritten coaching rule in the town to this day that coaches abide by this route.

Under questioning, Mr McKenzie, a director of Southdown, stated that although their application was to be awarded the sole rights to run to the top, they were prepared to share the service equally with the Corporation.

The Corporation maintained that during the three weeks that Southdown had been running to the top, this had had a very detrimental effect on the takings of the seafront service.

The Corporation argued that the upkeep of the road was paid for by them so they should have running rights over it but the commissioners were not impressed by this argument. They argued that many excursion firms had been given licences to operate, including many ex-servicemen who on returning from the war had purchased war surplus vehicles and converted them to charabancs. These licences carried no restrictions, so the commissioners drew the conclusion that, as until then the Corporation were not concerned about the number of buses using that road, it would now be wrong to argue there would be too many.

The proceedings then turned to the matter of how the two concerns had operated the temporary service. The commissioners had stated that they wanted the two concerns to share the service at half-hourly intervals. Southdown had made known their intention to start their service at 20 minutes past each hour. The Corporation, however, decided not to run at 10 minutes to the hour, but on the hour, which meant they had 40 minutes' worth of passengers as opposed to Southdown's 20 minutes. The commissioners were not impressed by this and Mr Ellison and Mr Cannon, his assistant, were grilled over this. Their excuse was that the timetables were prepared in a great hurry as the service started the following day. Their situation did not improve when asked if their drivers completed the trip in 18 minutes, what their reaction would be. They said they would be taken off as an unfit person to drive a public service vehicle. It was subsequently pointed out to the manager that his timetable only gave the driver 18 minutes to complete the trip and then to wait for 12 minutes before doing the return trip. He apologised, but said that the actual trip took about 25 minutes. The inference was that if passengers saw a bus standing waiting to go back it would attract more passengers and the temporary licence stated that buses must only stop at the top long enough to set down and pick up.

It was then stated that the applications from Southern Glideway Coaches and Eastbourne Motor Coach Association had been withdrawn and were thus formally refused.

The commissioners then heard the case for Orange Luxury Coaches. They stated that they believed that the route should be operated by a single operator rather than shared between two or more. They were not in a position to be able to operate this regularly and therefore withdrew their application, but asked the commissioners to licence only one bus per hour so that the smaller companies that had operated excursions for many years would still be able to survive.

Chapman's case was the next one to be considered. They stated that if the commissioners thought that the stage carriage service should be a monopoly, their application should be given serious consideration. They had been operating the route since 1905, longer than any other applicants, and had built up a good reputation based on the good service offered. They also put forward that they had forty-six vehicles registered in Eastbourne, so were also the largest operator. They stated that they did not really want a stage carriage licence, but if one was to be awarded it should be awarded to them. However if it wasn't, then restrictions should be put on the licence so that the smaller, established excursion operators could continue to trade.

Southdown were asked if they would be willing to give up their excursion licence if they were successful in obtaining a stage carriage licence. This would give the smaller excursion businesses more trade. They said they would be willing to do this.

Summing up for the Corporation, Mr Majoribanks apologised for the breach of their temporary licence, but denied it was a wilful breach. He said that the Road Traffic Act 1930 would cause serious competitive competition to the Corporation and during the temporary trial when a Southdown bus had been going to the top of Beachy Head at about the same time as a Corporation bus was going to the foot, then passengers carried by them had fallen by up to 40 per cent. Before the Act, the Corporation were happy not to run to the top as it meant that smaller operators including ex-servicemen could earn a living from excursion traffic, but the situation had now changed and if a licence was to be issued, it should be to them. Turning to the argument over Upper Dukes Drive, he said that the Corporation had purchased the land to preserve it for the benefit of all the residents and spent much money on maintaining the road and would have to spend much more on improving it in the future, so they thought it was not an audacious claim that they should have the sole rights to run a bus service over it. With that in mind, he suggested that the Corporation have a claim far above that of Southdown.

Mr Tylor, who summed up for Southdown, said he thought that the public would be better served if the licence was awarded to one company, but would be prepared to share the route if necessary. Southdown had been operating to the top since 1908 by excursions but the 1930 Act stated that regular services must be run by stage carriage and if they did not obtain the licence they would be losing business that had been theirs for over twenty years. Eastbourne Corporation, under the 1902 Act, had the right to operate to the top, but had chosen not to for their own reasons, but he thought they should not have the right to deny Southdown of their business now. He then made the point that if the Corporation had lost traffic on their seafront

service to the buses going to the top, then that was an admission that they had not been supplying a service that the public desired. As to the upkeep of the road, it was no different to any
other road. They were obliged to maintain all roads within the borough and that one was no
different to any other.

The commissioners then adjourned to come to their decision. On returning they said that
they thought undoubtedly there was a need for excursions and a stage carriage service. They
then went on to say that they had heard evidence from various parties saying that the service
would be better run by a single operator. As regards Chapman's, they not only had a good
reputation locally, but worldwide; however, they stated that they did not really want a stage carriage licence, but were more concerned that any other operator should not interfere with their
traffic at the pier. Their application was therefore refused.

Turning to Southdown, they acknowledged that they had been running a good excursion
service since 1908 and that the company was big enough and financially strong enough to
operate a good stage carriage service. Southdown had in 1908 applied to the Corporation to
run a stage carriage service to the top and had been turned down. In the past, parliamentary
committees had expounded the argument that if a local council had the authority to supply
a public service but declined to do so, and left private enterprise to risk its capital to build up
a service, then it was almost a principle that a local authority should not be allowed to step in
later and take that traffic. Southdown have also stated that in the peak month of August they
intended running sixty-two vehicle journeys each day, which was less than the number of
excursions operated. This would decrease the total number of vehicle movements on the seafront – a point of major importance.

The Corporation's case as expounded by their manager, Mr Ellison, was that they would use
double-deckers and extend their service from the foot to the top of Beachy Head. But there
was some concern over the suitability of these on the road to the top, and if double-deckers
were not suitable, then their service using single-deckers could not cope in peak times. The
commissioners disputed the way in which Mr Ellison had worked out that they had suffered a
loss on their seafront service since the experimental service to the top was started and decided
to disregard his evidence. They could also not agree with the argument put forward about
Upper Dukes Drive that profits made from the bus service would go towards the upkeep of it.
It was no different to any other road.

They therefore refused the application to Eastbourne Corporation and awarded it to Southdown
subject to certain conditions. These were that only single-deckers were used, any passengers boarding along the front must travel to the top and must not be set down at points along the promenade
and that duplicate services must not be run. The last condition was that Upper Dukes Drive must
be used on the upward journey, but Meads Road must be used for the return journey.

Mr Majoribanks, for the Corporation, then said that they intended to appeal to the Ministry
of Transport and asked that the temporary licences should continue until the appeal had
been heard. Southdown objected to this on the grounds that the licences were temporary
and the granting of them should not prejudice the final outcome. The commissioners agreed
with Southdown and would not extend the temporary licences so the last day of service by
Eastbourne Corporation to the top was 10 August 1931. The appeal was never lodged.

The following year in November, Eastbourne Corporation again submitted an application to
run to the top of Beachy Head. Again this was turned down.

The Corporation unanimously decided to appeal this judgement. They said that they had
not appealed the original application in 1931 as they wished to wait to see what impact
Southdown's service would have on their takings.

They were also of the opinion that the new Act did not have the intention of taking away the
powers to be the sole transport undertaking as granted to them under the 1902 Act. Councillor

Addison stated that the Act stated that some of the commissioners were appointed by County Councils and Borough Councils and thought that this provision was made so that the commissioners would protect their interest. This appeal was lost.

The first case under the new Road Traffic Act came before the town's magistrates in January. A lorry came out of a side road in front of an approaching bus. The driver of the bus braked and swerved but just caught the tailboard of the lorry. The magistrates found the lorry driver guilty but declared that as damage was minimal, the lorry driver's licence would not normally be endorsed, but the Road Traffic Act left them no option. He was also fined 10s with 10s costs.

Another bus driver to fall victim to the courts was employed on stage carriage work between London and Eastbourne. He was caught breaking the 30mph speed limit on the A22 at Chiddingly by a police motorcyclist who clocked him at 40–42mph. In court, the driver said he had no idea he was going that fast, but said that he had a timetable to run to, and the 3 hours given to him to reach Eastbourne from London including six stops to pick up passengers was not enough, but if he could not keep on time, his employer would find someone who could. The court had certain sympathy with his situation, but fined him 10s nonetheless. They added, however, that they hoped that the Traffic Commissioners would take note of the case and take appropriate action when their licences came up for renewal.

In April the first set of traffic lights were installed in the town at the junction of Terminus Road and Cornfield Road. They were not called traffic lights, but automatic traffic controllers. The local paper marked the event by saying they worked like clockwork and called them a signal success. They continued by saying that four of these robots had been installed at the junction. They were turned on by the Chief Constable who watched them with admiring interest and had perfect confidence in them. They were described as having a red eye that blazes forth the warning 'STOP'. After about 36 seconds an amber eye appeared below the red one, which meant, 'Get ready to start'. This was followed by a green one that meant 'Go'. Simultaneously the robots flashed a red light to traffic approaching from the other direction. It was then stated that these brainy contrivances had an advantage over the policeman as they had eyes in the back of their heads and out of their sides as well. They also had three eyes to each face. The Chief Constable agreed that some motorists may not know the meaning of the amber light and was considering having the word 'Caution' painted on it. The lights were only operational between 9a.m. and 6p.m. and were not used at all on Sundays. Although about sixty other towns in the UK had traffic signals, it is believed they were all of American manufacture and the sets installed at Eastbourne were the first to be made by the English firm of Siemens.

An elderly lady won damages of £50 from the Corporation when a bus she was trying to board pulled away, throwing her to the ground. There were differing accounts from witnesses as to whether she was waiting at the stop when the bus pulled up or if she arrived at the stop as the bus was leaving. The jury of four men and four ladies found in her favour.

The Chief Constable was concerned that at the end of three routes, buses had to reverse around a corner in order to turn round. Although the conductors were issued with red flags to help with this, he was not satisfied and thought the procedures dangerous. He put forward proposals where buses could turn. Although these meant extending the routes in some cases, the council approved them. He also recommended that no public service vehicle should stop within 50ft of a busy junction or crossing, bus stops should not be opposite each other and buses should not stop on bends.

Southern Railway was approached to see whether an awning could be fitted to the station building to protect intending passengers from the elements.

Councillors stated that the majority of towns allowed councillors to travel free on their buses, so the good councillors of Eastbourne awarded themselves the same benefit.

The Traffic Commissioners informed the depot that conductors and drivers would have to be licensed. These licences would cost 1s and 2s 6d respectively and would be the prescribed deposit against the badge. If the badge was surrendered then the monies would be refunded. This was on top of the 5s driving licence fee paid for by the council.

In June the Leyland Titans were ready for inspection at Leyland's works and the opportunity was taken to interview the India Tyre and Rubber Co. Ltd. A three-year deal was struck with the tyre company with a 2.5 per cent credit given for prompt payment.

Sixteen Leyland Titans were in service and it was decided to purchase a spare engine so this could be fitted while others were being repaired, thereby keeping buses on the road. This engine cost between £350–400.

In October the manager reported that a Compression Ignition Engine (diesel) would soon become available. Several manufacturers had produced an engine and a close eye was being kept on developments

1932

Class distinction was still alive and kicking in Meads at the start of 1932. The Transport Manager was asked to use double-deckers on the Sunday evening service to Meads, as there was not enough room for the maids going to work on the single-deck buses.

After over fifty years of trading, the local firm of Chapman & Sons Ltd hit on hard times. This was caused by a combination of factors including terrible summer weather in 1931, but the main reason was the recently introduced Road Traffic Act and the introduction of Traffic Commissioners. At an extraordinary meeting of shareholders, it was agreed to sell the business to Southdown. At this meeting, the chairman stated they had had a very bad financial year due to the obsolescence of old coaches, very bad weather, and loss of agency bookings due to the railway companies declining to allow agents to book for motor companies. This led to the company's worst ever trading year and no improvement could be foreseen until the world recession came to an end. In addition the new Act was bought into operation in 1931 governing the running of coaches through all areas of England, Scotland and Wales. This had meant that his staff had to attend Traffic Commissioners' enquiries as far away as Perth and Aberdeen.

He then read from a Sunday newspaper as follows:

The Traffic Commissioners have been sitting for ten months. During that time they have dealt the greatest blow to public travel facilities and made the greatest number of unreasonable, incredibly childish restrictions that were ever recorded against officialdom. The full effect of their work is little realised. Before they started, motor coach transport was expanding rapidly. But as a result of their ruthless banning and restriction-making according to one of the highest road transport authorities in Britain, there will be 25 per cent fewer services this year than there were in 1930. This will mean 15,000 fewer men will be needed, £1,800,000 less profit will be made, £1,200,000 (less) will be spent on petrol, £400,000 less on tyres and repairs, £3,000,000 less on new coaches and 6,000 existing coaches will be rendered useless, millions fewer will be able to travel by coach owing to lack of facilities. Scarcely a single new coach has been ordered this year. The damage the commissioners are doing in their courts is untold. Frankly, with one or two exceptions, they know less about coaches than the people who travel in them.

The chairman continued:

Now ladies and gentlemen, that is the position and this is what they call England, the land of the free, how shall we extol thee, who are born of thee. There are 13 Traffic Commissioners sitting in this country, who tell us that although we have paid our licences, 'You cannot come over our roads'. The Act is robbing us of customers as well as causing us considerable expense when we were having to make economies.

He continued to inform shareholders that nothing had been put away from the profitable times to cover the bad times, so not only would no dividend be paid that year, but no dividend would be paid until that year's losses were cleared by future profits, which would be at least four years, so it would be better for investors to put money made from the sale of the company into more profitable ventures.

Not only did Southdown buy the vehicles and spares, but they also took over Chapman's garage in Cavendish Place, which they continued to use for about the next seventy years.

Chapman's were not the only local company to fold. Southdown also bought out Southern Glideway, Foards and Cavendish who all lost valuable traffic to the top of Beachy Head to Southdown's stage carriage service.

One trader thought he could carry on without complying with the law and advertised a coach trip to London without a licence. The owner, Hartington Motors, and the driver of the vehicle both found themselves in the dock after an inspector had seen a poster advertising the trip and kept an eye on the vehicle, JK1129. After he had seen the vehicle pick up at three separate locations, he stopped it.

Mr Pratt, representing the owners, tried to argue that it was a private trip and therefore a licence was not needed, but after interviewing the passengers it became clear that they did not know each other, they had all paid for the trip, so it was being run commercially. Mr Pratt argued that he did not understand the new law, as did many other coach owners, but he was told that ignorance of the law was no excuse and was given a fine.

A letter was printed in the local paper labelling the Traffic Commissioners 'Mandarins'. It went on to say that out of thirty-five appeals against their decisions, sixteen had been granted. The letter writer continued that it was somewhat difficult to appreciate the ideas and motives of the Traffic Commissioners who dealt out and cancelled each other's restrictions, licences, permissions and recommendations, but it was certain that that the freedom of the road had been filched from the public who created and maintained it. As for the Beachy Head route, he continued that the ratepayers of Eastbourne had actually been debarred from running their own vehicles over their own roads at a cost of thousands of pounds and granted this very valuable monopoly to a powerful and influential limited liability company. He thought that the Corporation should carry on running the buses, 'Damn the Consequences', so that the ratepayers who were paying the piper could enjoy the collection.

Mr Ellison, speaking at a Municipal Transport Conference, said he should like to say what he thought about the Traffic Commissioners without libelling anybody, but said it was a terrible thing when you could not do what you liked in your own house. The Bus Committee and Corporation had always done their best for Eastbourne. Through kindness towards the smaller operators, the Corporation was now not allowed to run a service to the top of Beachy Head.

One of the old Eastbourne Corporation bus bodies had found its way onto an allotment site at Robertsbridge, about 20 miles from Eastbourne, and was being used as a shed. The Eastbourne Corporation motif had not been painted out and this had come to the notice of the council. A man was despatched with paint and brush to paint over the sign.

The Corporation applied to the Traffic Commissioners again to be able to run services to the top of Beachy Head on the grounds that the revenue on their parade services had fallen since the service to the top had started. The commissioners were not satisfied that the two facts were connected and again refused the application. They also rejected the argument that most of the route was maintained solely by the ratepayers of Eastbourne and those same ratepayers had bought the Downs in order to attract visitors and that any profit from that venture should be shared by them and not by the shareholders of a private company. Their appeal was again rejected and the town was still banned from running its buses over their own roads.

Towards the end of the year, the Ministry of Transport published a paper known as the Salter Report. This report suggested that there should be massive increases in Motor Vehicle Licence fees. The Borough Surveyor told the council that these proposed increases would mean an extra £1,380 per year on his twenty-five vehicles and the Transport Department would be affected more adversely. The Transport Manager said that the tax on a Titan would rise from £179 to £445 p.a.

By May, the new Titan buses (76–80) were ready for inspection at the Leyland factory. Four weeks later they had been delivered and were in service.

1933

In February the Certificate of Fitness of the first closed double-deck was due to expire as this had been converted in 1927. The manager successfully argued that it would make economic sense to spend money on renewing its certificate so it could be used for at least one more summer.

The manager also informed the Bus Committee that he felt that it would not be long before diesel would soon be a competitor to petrol-engined vehicles.

Some conductors unfortunately still thought that they could get away with fiddling money from the Corporation, but another was caught and fined £25 and told if he defaulted on this fine, he would face three months in prison. This conductor was dismissed for dishonesty when it was discovered that he had his own printing press and he had been printing his own bus tickets to sell!

This picture shows how labour-intensive the body shop used to be. (Eastbourne Buses Ltd)

The staff successfully argued that staff transport should be supplied to them to take them home after the services had finished as those living a distance from the depot could not get home. This service continues to the present.

In September, quotes were sought for the first buses to be powered by diesel rather than petrol engines. In December, Leyland supplied a demonstrator bus that was powered by diesel.

The Road Traffic Act continued to keep the courts busy. In October, another local coach operator, Herbert Thorogood, pleaded not guilty to using his vehicle illegally. He was stopped by the law just after midnight bringing a private party back from a dance at Jevington, a small village just outside Eastbourne. The defendant told the policeman he did not need permission from the Traffic Commissioners for this trip, as it was a private party. It transpired that the persons on the coach were all employed at the York House Hotel or their friends and had gone for an out of season party. Although they had paid for the trip, they had paid the organiser rather than the defendant, who had hired the coach, and the fee did not depend on how well patronised the trip was. The magistrates, who were hearing the case, dismissed it.

1934

A request was received from the organisers of the RAC Rally to be able to use the depot as a service centre. They calculated that a maximum of 240 cars could be serviced if all the buses were removed. The request was denied.

The first ticket machine was tried in the town that would take over from the old bell punches. Six machines supplied by Siemens were tried at a cost of £33 10s each.

A canopy was installed at the railway station to give waiting passengers some protection from the elements. The Southern Railway charged the Transport Department for this addition but

Bodywork complete and being prepared for painting. (Eastbourne Buses Ltd)

said that an electric clock and seats at this point would have to wait pending further alterations. The clock was eventually installed in the summer of 1935.

In February Leyland were asked to quote for six Titans, being petrol-engined double-deckers fitted with torque converters. These were delivered later in the year, numbered 81–86, and gave good service.

The councillors passed a motion that all members of the council be issued with passes entitling them to travel free of charge on all Corporation omnibuses. In an editorial in the local paper, it was stated that the council 'has never made a bigger mistake in its history'. Some councillors argued against the passes, but the motion was carried by a majority of two. The Editor stated that they had no more right to the privilege of free transport than any other ratepayer and their decision put every council member in a most unpleasant and degrading position, and went on to question whether in the future the councillors would vote themselves free deckchairs, theatre seats or games on the tennis courts or bowling greens.

Criticism was not confined to the Editor. A correspondent thought that the ratepayers perhaps also should foot the bill for the shoes they wore while walking to and from the bus stops.

One councillor, Hasdell, returned his free pass saying that some offensive and uncalled for remarks made by certain aldermen and councillors towards the elected representatives of the ratepayers made it impossible to retain the pass and keep one's self-respect.

At the next council meeting the matter was raised again, and it was proposed that the passes were to be for use when on council business only. This met with a tied decision with twelve councillors voting for the amendment and twelve against. The Mayor cast his deciding vote against the motion and the councillors kept their passes for all journeys.

Advertising was proving to be fairly lucrative. In the previous year £1,300 was raised for advertisements on the buses, with a further £237 raised from adverts on tickets.

An offer was received to buy buses 1 and 6 for £25 the two. These were Leylands that had been purchased new in 1919. The same person also offered £1 10s for an open lorry and £4 10s for a closed lorry. These offers were considered to be insufficient. It was decided to convert one bus, No.6, to a lorry, converting it to pneumatic tyres, and scrap the other three vehicles. An improved offer of £15 was received from a London firm (G.J. Dawson) for bus 6 but this was still considered too low and the conversion took place.

The buses were still being painted by brush, but some spray-painting apparatus was demonstrated and quotations arranged.

1935

Smoking was as much of an issue in 1935 as it is today. The council had decided to allow smoking in all parts of the buses. This led to objections from many sources. One councillor said that criticism of the decision was not confined to those who thought smoking was a disgusting and degrading habit, but thought that children and invalids should be considered in this matter. Inhabitants of the town were not slow to vent their feelings through the local paper, as usual. One writer thought that it seemed a 'tall order that one individual should put up with the breath-blown filth of another's pipe or the irritating ashes of cigarettes just because the majority of the Bus Committee approve such infringements of natural rights.'

Another enlightened passenger quoted the Ministry of Transport rules that stated that passengers must not cause injury or discomfort to other passengers or that passengers should not soil or defile any part of a vehicle or soil the clothing of other passengers, suggesting the Corporation were bound to ban smoking on buses completely.

Leyland Titan TD3 in Churchdale Road. The firm of jewellers, Wm Bruford, advertising on the side still exists in Eastbourne, but Fremlins Ales has passed into history. (Robin Bennett)

The National Society of Non-Smokers also organised a meeting to protest against smoking in buses. One speaker said that Eastbourne had long had a reputation for preserving social amenities and that it came as a complete shock to find the Corporation's complete disregard of the non-smokers in the community. A resolution of protest was carried.

Vandalism is apparently not a modern phenomenon either. In January three bus windows were broken by schoolchildren. It was suggested that the Education Committee should be charged for the damage, although this was decided against, but a special effort was to be made to alter the behaviour of schoolchildren.

For the Jubilee celebrations, the parade buses were festooned with red, white and blue greaseproof paper together with bunting and shields. One bus was illuminated for a torchlight parade. Fares taken over the Jubilee weekend were up £300 and the staff were congratulated for the fine manner in which they contributed to the success.

Quotes were obtained and orders placed for four more Leyland Titan double-deckers. These would be fleet numbers 87–90.

The depot's old Morris van was replaced. A quote for £155 was obtained and accepted which was £8 cheaper than the current van cost five years previously.

Authorisation was obtained from the Bus Committee to buy an electric fuel pump to replace the hand-operated one at a cost of £105.

The depot was in need of a repaint, so at the end of the season, instead of laying staff off as usual, it was decided to keep them on to do the painting.

1936

The Transport Manager reported to the committee that twenty single-deckers were now obsolete and he needed six new double-deckers.

In February a London-based coach company, Valiant Direct Coaches Ltd, went to the High Court to force the Traffic Commissioners to show cause for their refusal to grant licences to issue single tickets on their express services from London to resorts on the south coast.

Their legal representative explained that they were allowed to issue return or period tickets from London, but not to issue a single ticket from the south coast. The veto about single tickets from the coast caused great inconvenience as coaches had to return to London in any case and parents fetching their children from school could not take their children home with them on the same coach. Another complaint was that they could not issue a return from the coast. Counsel argued that certain advantages had been granted to the company that eased the situation, but when the Southern Railway, who were shareholders in Southdown Services, appealed, these advantages were withdrawn. The Court ruled that the commissioners must explain their decision.

Southdown applied for a licence to run from any dancehall or place of public assembly to destinations within 6 miles of the Town Hall. Eastbourne Corporation opposed this as they maintained they already ran an adequate service. Their licence was granted but with conditions. These were that the services would not leave before 11.30p.m., that a minimum fare of 6*d* be charged and that no one would be set down within the borough boundary.

In April the Transport Committee recommended to the full council that six more Leyland Titan double-deckers be purchased. These were to be petrol-engined with torque converters at a cost of £1,520 each. The reasons for this recommendation were that similar buses already running in the fleet were giving good service and that these buses that had no gearboxes were preferable to the AECs that had fluid flywheels and epicyclical gearboxes. The difference in price of only £2 was negligible. Some councillors were not happy to accept the committee's recommendations. One councillor said there were 6,000 AECs running in different parts of the country and put forward a motion that six AECs should be purchased. This motion was defeated. Another amendment that a tender from Dennis Brothers be accepted was also defeated. A further amendment was then put forward that three Leylands and three AECs should be purchased. This was passed and three AECs, 91, 92 and 93, and three Leylands, 94, 95 and 96, were purchased.

Smoking was still causing arguments and a correspondent who called himself 'A male smoker' wrote the following:

> While I am not averse to ladies smoking in private, I really think they should draw the line at smoking in public vehicles. This week I was a passenger on a Corporation bus and the only persons smoking were two ladies who puffed away at cigarettes – and looked thoroughly uncomfortable – I don't believe either of them liked smoking. They thought they looked modern – whatever that may mean.

In March whilst a fitter was working on an engine, his electric inspection lamp burst, setting light to the Autovac fixed to the dashboard. The position looked ugly for a while as the petrol flames looked as if they might spread to another bus, but owing to vigorous efforts of the men, assisted by office staff, the fire was put out by means of foam extinguishers. The Fire Brigade were called within a minute of the fire being seen but the fire was extinguished before they arrived, although they were very prompt.

An electric fuel pump had been installed at a cost of £92 to replace a manually operated one. This had proved to be a great success and permission was given to replace the other pump.

The manager reported that the depot would be very cramped when the six new doubles arrived and asked for permission to sell ten old singles. Although these had been purchased in 1926 they were still in good running order. These were Leyland Lions 40–49.

A record number of passengers, 14,343,836, had been carried in the last financial year. This was an increase of 546,107 on the previous year, but profits had dropped by about £1,300 to £14,540, which was still classed as satisfactory by the Borough Treasurer. Another £2,500 had been allocated to the general rate fund making a total of £41,195 being contributed over the years.

1937

The Borough Engineer had been asked to call in at Churchdale Road depot with a view to drawing up plans for new offices adjacent to the depot in Southbourne Road, but when the plans came before the council they met with some disapproval. One councillor described the ground floor plan as 'palatial' and questioned the desirability of having a dance floor or recreation room complete with three full-size snooker tables on the first floor. The proposed building would have a frontage of 150ft in Southbourne Road with a depth of 43ft. The offices would have a floor space of 6,000sq. ft, which would mean enough space for forty-five to fifty employees given the average of 100–150sq. ft per clerk. In reality there were only twelve clerical staff. Other councillors defended the proposals, however, stating that most towns provided facilities like these for their busmen and this town should not be left behind. Another pointed out that the crews were entitled to a break by law and it was only right that they be given somewhere to spend this break. It was then pointed out that the crews already had a rest room that was adequate for their purposes and was bigger than Southdown's rest room that catered for more staff. The proposed extension met with the approval of the majority and was therefore carried.

It seems strange that while such elaborate and expensive plans were being discussed, the manager was badly in need of a new typewriter and had to get committee approval for a new one. He had trialled a rebuilt 18in Royal machine, which had given satisfaction. The price quoted for this was 16s 6d. The other two typewriters in the offices were over ten years old.

The ten single-deckers (50–59) purchased in 1928 were nine years old and it was decided they should be gradually replaced. Three Leyland Titans (1–3) were delivered in 1937 with three more (4–6) the following year.

The Bus Committee suggested that cheaper fares be offered to workers who were travelling in the middle of the day, when the buses were not fully utilised. When this was put before full council, there was some disapproval of this, saying that it could put the undertaking's finances into the red and they proposed to refer this to the town's Finance Committee. Some members thought it was wrong that the working man was contributing to the undertaking's profits, which went to subsidising the rates (£2,500 of the £4,000 profit was allocated to the general rate fund). Another councillor said that if this move put the undertaking into the red, then non-bus users would be subsidising bus users and this would also be wrong. His argument won the day and the scheme for cheap fares was dropped.

Smoking on buses was raised again and it was decided that as a higher percentage of buses were now double-deckers, that smoking should only be allowed on the upper decks.

The health of the crews was considered by the town's Medical Officer of Health. He found that conductors suffered more sickness than the drivers. He thought that this may be due to them breathing in more exhaust fumes. He also said that some provision should be made for them to have somewhere to wash their hands before eating their food!

The blacksmith had also been ill for some time. His health was not improving and due to the strenuous nature of his work, the question of a retirement allowance for him bearing in mind his long, zealous and faithful service to the Corporation was considered. He was pensioned off and it was decided to combine the blacksmith's job with that of the foundry worker. Whilst doing this it came to light that the blacksmith had still been receiving danger money of 2s 6d for fitting solid tyres. This allowance should have stopped as the fleet now all had pneumatic tyres.

The prospect of another war was on the horizon and air-raid precautions were being formulated. Special buses were being provided to carry nurses to and from Princess Alice Hospital.

Tenders were invited for five new doubles fitted with petrol or diesel engines.

The cost of petrol was rising and a third increase in prices that year cost a further £1,500.

In September George Penn started his apprenticeship in the engineering section. When I started work with the department in 1972 he had worked his way up to Works Foreman. He was just one of many men who had very long service records with the buses.

1938

The manager advised the committee to buy five more double-deck buses as quickly as possible, as he could foresee extreme difficulties in obtaining new buses in the coming year. His advice was taken and tenders were invited for five petrol-engined buses. These were to be AECs (6–10). They were ready for inspection by June.

By September offers had been invited for seven Leyland single-deckers that the department had for sale. These offers ranged from £11 to £20 each. The tyre contractors said the un-run mileage on the tyres amounted to £84. The book value of the buses was only £7 10s each, so it was recommended to sell them all, but the tyres would have to be paid for separately.

Over the years the department had responded positively to requests from charitable organisations for free buses, but it was now felt that the increase in these requests was beginning to be a burden on the business. The last request had been from F. W. Woolworth to transport a group of elderly people to a party arranged by them at the Town Hall. It was felt that in future these costs should be met from public funds rather than the buses accounts. The next request for a free bus came from the Journeymen Butchers Annual Conference and this was denied. The undertaking was also giving free transport to 123 disabled ex-servicemen and it was thought that this expense should be met from national funds.

A complaint was lodged with the council that the Chairman of the Bus Board, Cllr Harvey, had obtained a pecuniary advantage as an employee of the bus undertaking had done some private work for him. The details of the complaint were that the chairman owned a mushroom farm and a pipe needing about a hundred joints had to be constructed. The chairman approached Mr Ellison, who had released a welder to do the work. The investigation showed that Cllr Harvey had agreed that he would pay the employee all the time that the welder was working for him and the Transport Department would not be paying him for that time. This

One of three AEC Regents delivered in 1936, No.91 stands at the station. (Robin Bennett)

was undertaken during the winter when work was slack and the welder could be spared from his duties. More minor complaints of having the use of a department van and having part of a concrete mixer fixed at the depot were proved to be unfounded, as he had been invoiced for these matters.

Mr Ellison was also accused of having his car fixed at the depot and having an employee pick him up at Dover Docks when he returned from holiday. In his defence, he said that the council had agreed in the past that his car should be fixed at the depot and as for the member of staff picking him up, he said that he wanted to discuss with him what had been happening while he had been away, adding that if he had been the Managing Director of a public company, it would be normal practice and the shareholders would not complain.

All allegations of wrongdoing by Cllr Harvey and Mr Ellison were found to be baseless and no further action was taken.

The department continued to expand with record numbers of passengers, 14,795,102, and income of £81,708 being recorded.

Chapter 5

The Second World War Years

Percy Ellison retires; help with the war effort; service cuts; deaths in service

1939

Mr Ellison was due to retire on 30 April, but asked the committee if he could carry on for a year as he wished to see through some projects he had started. The committee rejected his request, however, and advertised for a replacement to start on a salary of £550. Mr Ellison was not even allowed to stay on for three months to help the new manager and assist with air-raid precautions. He was retired on a pension of £280. Mr Ellison argued that although he had bought his own car, it was maintained at the depot and he said that this money for maintenance was part of his salary which meant that his salary should have been £103 p.a. more meaning his pension should be increased accordingly. He won the argument and his pension was increased to £308.

There were seventy-five applicants for the post of General Manager. Six were shortlisted and interviewed. The successful applicant was a Mr John Atherton, who had been General Manager and Engineer at Leigh Corporation Transport Department.

The council paid tribute to Mr Ellison who had built up the undertaking from a concern that carried just over 1,000,000 passengers in 1904–5 to nearly 15,000,000 in 1937–8. The total profit had amounted to £125,863 of which £47,706 had been contributed to the general rate fund.

Mr Ellison had offered £120,000 to buy the undertaking. He was serious about the offer as he thought there was a possibility of it being sold or a working arrangement made with another concern and that would prove the thin end of the wedge. He went on to say, 'God help you fellows if this undertaking is ever sold to a private undertaking.'

Mr Ellison was not the only long-serving member of staff to retire that year. Chief Inspector John Wise also retired after serving for thirty-six years. He had been with the undertaking since its inauguration, and had served as chief inspector for thirty-four years. Mr Wise died two years later.

In May there was a large ARP practice in Eastbourne. A scenario was enacted of a large bomb having exploded in the Seaside area of the town. Casualties were played by Air Cadets. One single-deck bus was converted into an ambulance and arrived at the scene fitted with ten stretchers. Another single-deck bus arrived soon afterwards. This bus had been fitted out as a first aid centre.

Blackouts were in force and neither buildings nor vehicles were allowed to display any lights. This proved to be very dangerous and before the end of the year, an old-age pensioner was hit and killed by a Corporation bus. A verdict of accidental death was recorded. The coroner said that in these times the onus on safety fell more on the pedestrians as, whilst someone in dark clothes was perhaps invisible to a motorist, never at any time is a motor vehicle quite invisible to a pedestrian.

In November, the department received a letter from the Ammunition Production Department asking for details of their plant. This was with a view of starting of the manufacture of arms at the depot.

The three Dennis one-man-operated vehicles were withdrawn from service. One was retained for sundry transport work for the present emergency. The remaining two were stripped of magneto, dynamo, carburettors and glass. Mr Atherton submitted an offer of £6 for the remains of each vehicle but it is not clear what he wanted them for.

Seven old Leyland Lions were being stored at the depot. Subject to Ministry of Health approval, six of these would be needed by the Air Raid Precautions Committee (four would be converted into ambulances and two into mobile first aid units). The other had already been converted into an ambulance for inter-hospital transport at a cost of just under £20, which had been charged to the ARP Committee, but no charge had been made for the purchase of the vehicle or its tyres.

Four long-term employees were due to retire and they were entitled to 1/120 of their wages for every year worked This meant pensions ranging from 7s 3d per week for fifteen years to 13s 1d per week for twenty-three years service.

The war was having an effect on the bus service in other ways. A 9p.m. curfew was put on the buses under a new regional order. Under the same order, Sunday services would not start until 1p.m. The Transport Commissioner appealed to the public to accept these restrictions as necessary in the public interest and to co-operate as far as possible by using services considerably earlier than the last one shown in the timetable. People were reminded that all fuel used in this country had to be imported in tankers that had to run the gauntlet of submarines and long-range bombers.

The commissioner was asked that a small extension to the curfew be granted so that the passengers arriving on three trains between 9p.m. and 9.30p.m. could get home. The commissioner refused this request and those passengers had the unenviable task of walking home in the pitch black.

Buses were being damaged in air raids. AEC Regent No.91 had some windows blown out on 13 September 1939 and Leyland Titan TD3 suffered similar damage two days later.

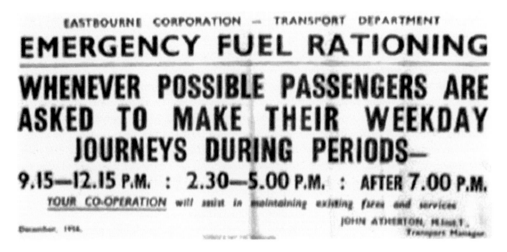

Poster asking passengers to stagger their journey times. (Eastbourne Buses Ltd)

1940

The manager was given permission to buy an oil filter so that old oil could be re-used. This was essential during wartime. The cost of the equipment would be £82 from Equipment & Engineering Co. Ltd, but this paid for itself over time.

An off-duty conductor was killed in an air raid, and a fatal accident occurred to a pedestrian on 2 November. A verdict of accidental death was reached. The driver was exonerated from all blame and the coroner expressed sympathy for the driver. It was very dangerous walking the streets at night with neither streetlights nor headlights on vehicles being allowed.

On the code word 'CARCAN' the whole depot was to be evacuated to Golden Cross, about 15 miles out of town. The following message was prepared and copied ready to be handed to ten bus drivers. All ten of these messages still exist in the company archives, complete with the list of ten drivers that they were to be delivered to. The fact that they still exist is proof that they were never needed:

EASTBOURNE CORPORATION MOTOR OMNIBUS DEPARTMENT.
EMERGENCY,
Please report to the Motor Omnibus Depot as quickly as possible for the purpose of taking our buses, as directed by the Military, to a point in the countryside.
If possible you should bring an emergency supply of food, sufficient for at least 12 hours, knife, fork, spoon, and mug, a blanket (or blankets) and overcoat, shaving materials and any other necessary clothes and kit you think you might require to cover an absence of several days. Also your gas mask, identity card and ration cards. (If you are a conductor, bring your cash bag, punch and other kit).
All vehicles must be filled with petrol before leaving the depot.
A GAP OF AT LEAST 170 YARDS MUST BE ALLOWED BE EACH VEHICLE TRAVELLING ON THE ROADS,
PLEASE TREAT THIS AS A MATTER OF NATIONAL URGENCY.
J.
General Manager & Engineer,
Driver Walker.   Eastbourne Corporation Motor
Omnibus Department.

A grateful passenger, Mrs M. Bell, sent every employee of the bus undertaking who was serving in the forces a Christmas present. She sent thirty-two presents in all and had received twenty-six replies from the grateful recipients. She said that the men had served the town so well that she wanted to give them something as a token of her appreciation. Some of the presents sent were games like dominoes to help them pass the time.

In November a headline appeared in the local paper saying 'Bus Hurled over Hedge By Bomb'. Reporting restrictions prevented an exact location and details from being printed. It was reported that it was a single-decker making its way along a country lane, so presumably it was a Southdown or Maidstone and District. The blast picked the bus up, spun it round in the air and over a hedge with the vehicle finishing up on its side in a field facing the way in which it had come. Four people were killed, including the conductor, but miraculously the driver survived. He had to kick out a cab window to escape, after which he helped with the rescue of other passengers.

1941

On 1 February a brightly coloured bus hit the streets of Eastbourne with the approval of the Bus Committee. It was still in the traditional blue and yellow livery but in brighter shades. Mr Atherton said he thought it would give the right touch of colour and when peace arrived it would show visitors that Eastbourne's reputation for smartness had not been dimmed by the war. Mr Atherton's views on the colour scheme were not universal though. One correspondent to the local paper, who signed himself 'Dazzled', wrote to say he had never seen a more bilious combination of colours in his life. He thought that apart from being an obvious target for enemy machine-gunners, he considered it quite out of keeping with the dignity of the town. He went on to say that he thought in some drab industrial centre in the Black Country or in the North there might be an excuse for this kind of garish decoration, but not in Eastbourne.

Despite other objections, including one that said that the original colours were the colours of the Duke of Devonshire who owned large areas of the town, the council agreed that the new colour scheme would stay.

Many conductors had been granted leave of absence without pay because their services were not required. There was now a shortage of conductors and the manager was instructed to tell these men to report back for duty. It was pointed out that some of these men had taken other jobs that were helping in the war effort and the long-term future of these men should not be jeopardised if they stayed with their present employer. The committee stated that they would rather employ these men if they were available than resort to employing women conductors.

A regular bus user wrote to the newspaper complaining about the number of old bus tickets that were discarded at bus stops. He thought that in order to keep the town tidier, these tickets should be collected and recycled. He concluded that even an insignificant thing such as a discarded bus ticket can make a difference these days and ended with the saying, 'Many a mickle makes a muckle.'

A casualty of war opposite the railway station. Miraculously it was re-bodied and put back into service. A body lies under the bus at the back. (Eastbourne Buses Ltd)

1942

At this time, Eastbourne had been declared a Defence Area. This meant that only those persons with a pass could enter the town. A lady who was holidaying in East Grinstead fell foul of this ruling when she thought she would have a day out in Eastbourne by bus. When her Southdown bus arrived at Langney Green at the eastern end of the town, it was boarded by a policeman, who checked the passengers' passes. Unfortunately for Mrs Humphreys she didn't have the appropriate documents and was asked to leave the bus and to catch the next bus back. She did get her wish to visit Eastbourne though as she was summoned to appear in court for her actions! The irony of the situation was not lost on the court and the magistrates dismissed the summons under the Probation of Offenders Act.

The bus stops immediately outside the station were moved as a matter of safety, as this was regarded as a target for bombers and the stops were under a glass canopy. This brought more letters of complaint from the good people of Eastbourne as well as one or two that congratulated the manager on his good sense and foresight.

1943

Eastbourne had a ban on advertising on the seafront and some councillors thought that this should apply to the seafront buses as well. It was pointed out that sometimes relief trips had to be run and a spare supply of buses without advertising on would have to be kept for this purpose. It was decided that this would be impractical, so advertising on seafront buses was allowed to continue.

1944

In February, road safety awards were handed out to the staff. The scheme was run by the Royal Society for the Prevention of Accidents (as it still is). Eight men received awards for completing fifteen consecutive years of safe driving while others received lesser awards. The Mayor attended the ceremony held in the staff canteen, where he told the members that in the past year 553,932 miles were operated and 5,929,939 passengers were carried; despite this the total cost of all the accidental damage sustained by the buses was just £2.

In 1944 a group of busmen got together and decided to compile a newsletter to send to those serving in the forces. Members of the forces were kept up to date with their friends back home and forces' addresses of others serving elsewhere were published so they could keep in touch with each other. There was at least one poem published in each newsletter and I reproduce one below:

How I'd like to be a bus
For if some disrespectful cuss
Drops a bomb or something near
It needn't have a lot of fear
Concerning damaged body or face
We send it to a northern place
And then within a month or two
The bus returns as good as new
Seventy five and sixty four
Are out upon the road once more

To the satisfaction of us all
The utility changes are quite small
While Eddie was driving home the latter
He thought that something was the matter
For it rocked and swayed a bit
What d'you think was wrong with it?
To Cyril's eyes At once 'twas clear
The two front wheels were at the rear!

In August it was considered safe to revert back to the usual stopping places outside the station, nearly two years after they had been moved to West Street, about 100 yards away.

In October, improved services were put in to cope with the return of many residents to the town. This was done with the approval of the Regional Traffic Commissioner, who stated that the lifting of the curfew on late-night buses was being considered by the Government and he hoped to be able to give more information on this in the near future. Two weeks later, he did announce that the curfew was lifted and the department immediately started running services up to 10.30p.m.

In December, Percy Ellison died, aged seventy-three. A guard of bus employees led by the chief inspector formed outside the church at Westham where the service was held.

1945

Mr Atherton gave an assurance to those men who had been employed as bus conductors since the start of hostilities that they would not lose their jobs when the regular men were demobilised. Approximately fifty men would soon be released from the forces, but the future was not as bleak as it looked. Although he could not make a definite promise, he thought it extremely unlikely that any men would be stood off.

The war years had not improved the behaviour of some sections of society, as at the end of 1945 there was a spate of seat slashing. Petty pilfering was also happening and seventeen light-bulbs were taken during a one-week period.

A councillor drew the committee's attention to an amusing incident that happened to him. He was on a bus in the town centre when a man carrying a long roll of linoleum boarded. Unfortunately the man rested the roll against the bell push and the driver pulled away, leaving many passengers and the conductor behind!

It was decided to fit heaters in five of the new buses on order. This was met with some opposition as one councillor declared that people who travelled by bus went prepared for all weathers and did not need mechanical aids to keep warm. His views were backed up by a fellow councillor who declared that it was unnecessary to install heaters when local journeys were so short. The committee were told that it cost £32 to buy and install a heater, but the running cost was zero as they operated from the engine. Luckily, the majority of councillors were more sympathetic to the passengers' needs and the decision to install heaters went ahead.

A fifteen-year-old girl was fined 10s by juvenile magistrates for unlawfully giving the driver the signal to leave. The court heard that as she was walking upstairs she leant over and rang the bell. There was an elderly lady boarding behind her and when the driver pulled away, she was thrown to the ground and injured. In her defence, the girl said she knew the conductor and thought it would be all right to ring the bell. She did not see anyone boarding behind her. Her mother said she thought it was time the practice of ringing bells was stopped, having been on a bus a few days beforehand when a passenger rang the bell, leaving the conductor behind.

In December at a transport-men's thanksgiving service, the Revd F. Macintosh told his congregation of an incident at the station when a driver of a Corporation bus full of passengers saw a bomb, released from an enemy aircraft, heading towards him. He accelerated as hard as he could and managed to get his bus and passengers to safety as the bomb exploded behind him.

He continued by saying that all the men who had left the buses to fight in the war had returned safely, but unfortunately declared that three employees had been killed in the town. He was also thankful that the depot had not been blown to smithereens.

One of the few things that were cheaper than pre-war prices was bus travel and even after five years of war the public enjoyed a cheaper and more efficient bus service than in any other country. The number of passengers had increased by between 30–50 per cent on pre-war levels. This was despite the fact that numerous vehicles had been requisitioned by the Government. Meanwhile maintenance costs had soared. Spares had gone up by 40 per cent, fuel by 50 per cent and lubricating oil by 80 per cent, yet fares had remained stable. Companies, though, were facing massive bills for new buses, as it was estimated 20,000 new vehicles were needed across the country.

Chapter 6

The Post-Second World War Years

Getting back to normal; nationalisation; integration with Southdown

1946

In March, Southdown resumed their long-distance services. Two luxury services left Eastbourne and arrived safely at Victoria Coach Station.

A luncheon was given at the coach station to celebrate the resumption of services. The Managing Director of Southdown Motor Services Ltd, Mr A. Cannon, made a speech in which he criticised the Government's plans to nationalise coach services. He quoted a Government spokesman saying that the idea behind nationalisation was to give the public an efficient service, but denied that his services were inefficient. Another Southdown official, Mr Carling, stated that Southdown owned 705 vehicles. Three hundred and thirteen of these were coaches, but the Government had compulsorily acquired 121 for use by the armed services and so far only ten had been returned. This was leading to operational problems and, although the company were trying to get back to pre-war levels, many duplicate services would not be able to run.

Lack of hotel accommodation was making long-distance tours impossible, but vehicles that would normally have been used on these tours were being used elsewhere.

He said that their coaches that had been commandeered for the war effort had been used for varying work, including the conversion for ambulance work, conveying unequipped military units, and providing emergency substitutes for the rail network.

The number of standing passengers on buses, which had been increased to twelve during the war, was reduced by Parliament to five. Charles Taylor, MP for Eastbourne, opposed this as he contended that the same abnormal conditions existed as during the war.

Southdown were having trouble in coping with the numbers of passengers during the evening rush hour and the police were needed to control the crowds that queued three deep for long distances at the Pevensey Road bus depot. Although extra buses were run, it was 8p.m. before the numbers of intending passengers were cleared.

Eastbourne Corporation was not faring much better. They only had forty-four buses, compared with the pre-war total of fifty-nine. Eleven new buses were on order though, and tenders had gone out for a further eight. However, the chairman warned that it would be 1948 before all these buses could be delivered. There was a bottleneck at the body-builders, but Eastbourne was top of the list for the next ones to be built.

In December, a reporter looked into the problems of the passengers and came to the following conclusions:

The first double-decker to be delivered after the war was No.19, a Wehmann-bodied AEC that served in the town for twenty years, being used as a driving school bus near the end of its life. (Eastbourne Buses Ltd)

– Too many schoolchildren riding at half fares at peak times.
– Although the children only travel short distances, it nevertheless prevents workers from getting on the buses in between the main stages.
– Too few buses at peak periods.
– No provision is made for additional transport on rainy days when needs are particularly heavy.

1947

In January the council decided not to co-operate with the British Omnibus Companies Public Relations Committee in its opposition to the Transport Bill, which was then before Parliament. The Town Clerk was instructed to inform the committee that although the council were not opposed to nationalisation, they were against the fact that, as it stood, the Bill gave local authorities no compensation whatsoever. It was pointed out that railway stockholders would receive Government stock in return and road transport owners were assured at least of their goodwill and livelihood and were generous to the extreme compared to local government.

A strange accident happened in March. Two elderly ladies had to be taken to hospital after a horse smashed its head through a closed window of a bus in the town centre. The horse belonged to the Southern Railway and was being led to its stables when it suddenly took fright and veered into the bus. The ladies suffered from severe shock, while the horse needed ten stitches in its nose.

1948

Southdown approached Eastbourne Corporation with a suggestion that they should combine services. Discussions between the two undertakings had been ongoing for about a year and in January Mr Atherton presented a report to the council on the matter. The following are extracts from his report.

Southdown referred to the Portsmouth area where they had combined their services successfully with Portsmouth Corporation. The financial side of the merger was worked out by combining the takings and mileage of both concerns and then splitting the revenue in proportion to the mileage run by both parties. Although the system was working well in Portsmouth, Mr Ellison said that different factors applied in Eastbourne. Portsmouth was on a peninsula with only one route into it, so there was no fanning out of routes. The town's housing stock had sustained heavy damage during the war with 7,000 being totally destroyed and 50,000 out of 65,000 being badly damaged. The population could not all be re-housed in the city centre and had scattered to the outskirts and Portsmouth Council were seeking to obtain a large area of land for housing estates from Hampshire County Council. Portsmouth City Council had applied to run services to these new areas, but Southdown objected and it was, in fact, Portsmouth Council that had approached Southdown with a view to a merger. These circumstances did not apply in Eastbourne. Development in Eastbourne is slow as the sea is to the south, Beachy Head and the protected South Downs lie to the west and the Crumbles and marshland lie to the east, so transport requirements cannot speedily change.

Another reason to merge could be the talk of nationalisation. Southdown claimed that if the two concerns were merged, the British Transport Commission would have no grounds to acquire transport in this area. Mr Atherton did not agree with this view. He said it was a fact that the Commission had acquired nearly all of Brighton, Hove and District and if they did not acquire Southdown, they would show no interest in Eastbourne Corporation. If, however, Southdown were taken over and Eastbourne Corporation were linked with them, the same process would automatically apply to Eastbourne.

As an independent operator, with no outside links except to the railway, they were not a necessity to any comprehensive scheme of transport and as long as they retained their independence they had freedom of action in all negotiations. In connection with any British Transport Commission Scheme put forward, they had to be consulted twice: first as a County Borough and afterwards as a transport operator. All such schemes must go through a legal process and he could not visualise anything affecting them arising during the life of the present parliament. He thought that complete nationalisation was inevitable, but the process would be slow and added that a small independent operator like theirs would not be high on their agenda. He therefore advised the council against proceeding with the scheme.

A notice to staff in May warned conductors of the dangerous practice of changing the side blind by holding onto the grab rail on the platform and leaning out whilst turning the handle to wind the destination to the correct place. A conductor had sustained injuries that could have proved fatal. Conductors were threatened with disciplinary action if they were caught breaking this rule.

The rules on standing passengers were altered to allow eight instead of five standing passengers to be carried, providing all the seats were taken. Some conductors were taking the ruling literally and making passengers climb the stairs rather than stand inside. This led to an elderly lady, who had never been upstairs on a bus before, having an accident whilst climbing the stairs. The conductors were asked to act sensibly and be flexible when imposing this rule, as it would lead to safer travel and fewer arguments.

Annual outings for staff were allowed and paid for by the council. Most years this included a trip to the Commercial Motor Show. Many staff wanted to attend so two trips were organised,

AEC Regent III, fleet No.30, at the pier. (Eastbourne Buses Ltd)

so the running of the town's service was not affected by staff shortages. The council also awarded the staff a 4*s* meal allowance for these trips.

Buses 66, 67, 68 and 70 were sold for £35 each, while 74 realised £70.

It was decided to tender for chassis for eight new double-deckers and one new single. A contract already existed with East Lancashire Coach Builders Ltd to supply the bodies.

1949

The Crossley buses (32–39) already on order had increased in price to £2,078 each making a total of £16,624, an increase of £748. The Transport Manager had to ask permission from the Minister of Transport to borrow the extra money.

A councillor put forward the idea that uncollected fare boxes or 'conscience boxes' be fitted to the buses. The idea was initially rejected but he persevered, asking that six be fitted to routes with frequent stops. This idea was taken up, and presumably the money collected in the boxes was worth having as it was decided to equip the rest of the fleet with them.

Organisations applied to be given a bus for free for various reasons. Buses were given to the branch managers of a well-known travel agency who were guests of the town, the New Zealand cricket team who were staying in town and the Southern Counties Touring Society, but the poor Salvation Army who requested one to go carol-singing in were made to pay 12*s* 6*d* to cover the staff costs involved.

Tenders were received for the eight new chassis (41–48). These were from Leyland Motors (£1,734), Guy Motors Ltd (£1,745), AEC Ltd (£1,751), Crossley Motors Ltd (£1,793), Fodens Ltd (£1,938), and Transport Vehicles (Daimler) Ltd (£1,947). The General Manager recommended that the offer from AEC be accepted, both for these doubles and the one single-decker.

1936 AEC Regent III converted to a breakdown vehicle in 1949. (Paul Redmond)

A tender was also put out for the bodywork of the single-decker and four tenders were submitted from Welsh Metal Industries Ltd (£1,800), East Lancs (£1,970), Crossley Motors Ltd (£1,990) and Brush Coach Works (£1,990), with the East Lancs offer being accepted.

Much work had been done by the Town Clerk, the Borough Treasurer and the General Manager on talks that had gone on with Southdown on co-ordination of services and the Transport Committee was informed of the talks so far and asked for their permission to progress further. The committee though were against these talks and said that no further action should be taken.

By June the eight Crossleys had been delivered and this meant that some of the older vehicles could be disposed of. It was agreed to scrap 1934 Leyland Titan No.81 but to convert four earlier 1932 Leylands (77–80) to open-toppers. The top to No.80 was used as a bicycle shed.

In September it was decided to sell Leyland Nos 69 and 71. Four offers were received with bids ranging from £20 to £105 and the top bid from Carricrop Trailers was accepted. No.76 was scrapped.

A local fisherman was granted permission to buy an old engine that had been lying around the depot for a while. It is not clear whether this went on to power a boat or, more likely, was used as a winch to pull boats up the beach.

1950

In January, the staff were told that six new drivers would be needed for the summer service and that the department was willing to train conductors to be drivers and those interested should apply.

The undertaking continued to be profitable, with the year ending April 1950 making a net profit of £22,325. £5,000 of this was transferred into the General Rate Fund.

The depot had suffered a lot of bomb damage during the war and this was still being fixed. Whilst this work was being undertaken more routine work was identified as necessary on the roof gutters and the manager had to ask for permission to outlay another £215 to remedy this.

Revenue continued to be gained from advertising. A company called Darby's had been used for many years, but this year the undertaking renegotiated its terms to be more favourable. Two thirds of all revenues from advertising would be returned to the department with a minimum of £2,000 per year being received. The advertising company seemed to be set on promoting unhealthy products with beer being the favourite. Perhaps the thinking was that if their campaigns were successful, then those over-indulging in their products would be unable to walk home and therefore have to catch a bus!

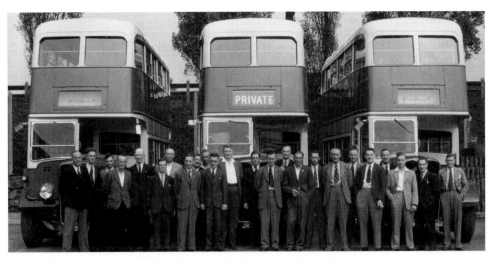

Three AEC Regent IIIs ready to leave the factory in 1947. (Eastbourne Buses Ltd)

In June, drivers were told that the increase in the price of fuel was going to wipe out any profit, so fuel conservation was paramount. As all the buses now had self-starters, engines had to be switched off at terminal points and the town centre.

Petrol had come off rationing in May 1949 and the General Manager asked to revert to the pre-war practice of tendering for the bulk supply of diesel, petrol and lubricating oils.

Bus 84 was sold to Escort Coaches for £65, while 85 and 97 went to Lammas Motors Ltd for £50 each.

In order to stop the dangerous practice of intending passengers jumping onto moving buses by grabbing the handrails at the rear of the bus, the Transport Manager decided to remove the handrails of buses 19, 27 and 38 and place them inside the vehicle. This seemed to make little difference as no more buses were converted.

In November the department was approached by the resettlement officer of the 7th Tank Regiment asking if they could be of any help in retraining army personnel to become bus drivers, but his request was denied.

1951

A loss was estimated for the year of about £20,000. This was due mainly to the increase in the price of fuel in the last budget of 9d per gallon, costing £9,000 over the course of the year and a further increase in the present budget of 4½d. The manager told the Transport Committee that fares would have to rise and among other things this led to the abolition of all halfpence fares.

In June the Omnibus Society was treated to a guided tour of the workshops and a free trip around the town.

In September Metropolitan-Cammell-Weymann offered on a free two- to three-week loan of a Leyland Olympic single-deck vehicle. This was a chassis-less bus, having its engine mounted underneath, with an overall length of 30ft and width of 8ft, capable of carrying forty-four passengers.

Despite the financial problems of the undertaking, two local councillors asked the department to give free fares to old-age pensioners. A similar request was received from Eastbourne Voluntary Association for the Care of Cripples. Both requests were denied, saying that it was not the undertaking's place to subsidise fares.

AEC Regent III No.30 poses at Willingdon village, possibly for the inauguration of a new service. (Eastbourne Buses Ltd)

1952

The tyres continued to be hired rather than purchased and tyre companies Michelin, India, Dunlop, Pirelli, Goodyear, Firestone and Avon all tendered the same amount of 1.03*d* per car mile. The committee thought that all these tenders were too high and instructed the manager to renegotiate. Surprisingly all companies re-tendered for exactly the same amount again – 0.84*d* per mile. The India Tyre and Rubber Co. Ltd were awarded the contract.

The depot was allowed to expand using land that became available due to four houses that were destroyed during the war.

Southdown wanted to divert their service to Heathfield through Willingdon village rather than going straight up the A22. This led to objections from the undertaking with the Traffic Commissioners and more bad feeling between the two companies. Perhaps the talks that were going on in 1949 should have been allowed to continue. The Transport Manager gave details of many routes he wished to alter to meet the needs of the expanding town. It was agreed to lodge objections to any variation or developments proposed by Southdown which would adversely affect the town's services.

1953

A celebration lunch was held to commemorate the department's Golden Jubilee. The guest of honour at the Devonshire Lawns restaurant was the original Transport Manager, eighty-six-year-old Mr John Brydges. He held the reins for two years before handing over to Mr Ellison. He recalled relieving a driver for his lunch, when he drove his bus from the town centre to the Archery and back. He was proud of the fact that he did not have an accident, as he had never driven a bus before!

A driver, George Cottington, who had driven buses in Eastbourne for forty-seven years, recalled in the early days when drivers carried an assortment of nuts and bolts as well as a spare

In April 1953, to commemorate the department's fiftieth anniversary, Leyland Lion No.12 was specially decorated and contained an exhibition of photographs, models and other exhibits. It toured the town, stopping at various places. The crown on the roof was illuminated at night. The two model buses on the roof still exist. (Eastbourne Buses Ltd)

spark plug and rubber tubing to fix fuel leaks. He continued that a wheel cap would sometimes fall off and anyone finding it would be given a reward of threepence, which the conductor would pay from his bag. George retired later in the year and it is estimated that he drove about 850,000 miles and carried between 9 and 10 million passengers.

The Chairman of the Transport Committee, Mr H. Archer, also reminisced that in the early days, it was not unusual for passengers to be asked to get out and push the bus up slopes and that was a task he had performed many times in the past.

Group shot of guests attending the fiftieth Jubilee lunch on the steps of the Devonshire Lawns restaurant. (Eastbourne Buses Ltd)

During the first fifty years the department had grown a great deal. From four buses in 1903, they now operated fifty-seven. In the first year of operation 430,000 passengers were carried, compared with 18 million in 1952. The service could then cater for up to 75,000 passengers every day and transport the entire population of Eastbourne in 12 hours.

1954

Vandalism continued to be a problem. A notice to staff in 1954 stated that four buses had had their seats slashed and urged conductors to be on the lookout for the perpetrator.

Trams actually arrived in Eastbourne in 1954, but they were not to serve the public on the town's roads. These would be a tourist attraction and would be miniature, rather than full size. The route went from the gates of Princes Park at the east end of the town taking a circular route over the Crumbles (an area of shingle, which was once under water). It was operated by Modern Electric Tramways of Barnet. The trams were the idea of a Mr Claude Lane, whose business was manufacturing light electric road vehicles. He built a miniature tram for his own amusement, which he used to take to local fêtes where it aroused great interest. Before the tramway was built in Eastbourne, the company ran a similar operation in Rhyl, North Wales. To help persuade the powers-that-be in Eastbourne that this was a good idea, a short section of track was laid in Eastbourne and two of the trams were transported from Rhyl to give a demonstration. This proved successful, and permission was given to go ahead with the project.

Construction of the track started in May, and workshops and shed to house the trams were built near the end of Wartling Road.

One of the town's trams near the terminus at Princes Park. (Eastbourne Buses Ltd)

1955

Until 1955, destination blinds did not display a route number, although the town's publicity department had been urging this for some time. A decision was originally taken that route numbers would be displayed on the front panels only, but this was changed to include all blinds at a cost of £495. A prototype blind was manufactured and shown to the Transport Committee for approval in April, and by August the fleet had been fitted.

Although the department was short of staff, its adverts for bus conductors still stipulated that only males need apply. Following in Mr Ellison's politically incorrect footsteps, when he said he would not be responsible for the public's safety if women were allowed to drive, Mr Atherton said they were not considering employing women conductors yet. He went on to say that:

> The situation is not as desperate as that, but we may reach that stage. There's no telling. They're pretty tough. They do a good job of work and we have no objection to women at all, but we do not think it is a good policy to mix men and women conductors in a small undertaking.

Southdown celebrated forty years of service in Sussex. They had been formed from an amalgamation of three companies: Brighton, Hove and Preston United Omnibus Company; Worthing Motor Services; and London & South Coast Haulage Company. They were operating about 1,000 buses and employed 4,000 men.

The Transport Committee recommended to the full council that a new office block should be built attached to the present depot, that two new buses be purchased in 1955, four buses be bought in 1956–7 and four more in 1957–8 (although this would be subject to review).

It was decided to dismantle the last two petrol-engined buses and use them for spare parts. These were two of the open-top fleet. It was thought that there would be no point in trying to sell these buses, as there was no market for petrol buses anymore. These open-toppers would be replaced by converting three pre-war double-deckers during the winter and purchasing three new buses to replace these. These would arrive in February, followed by four more in April.

1956

In April a letter appeared in the *Eastbourne Chronicle* accusing the buses of causing TV interference. The Post Office confirmed this and said the problem was due to fans on heaters. Letters appeared in subsequent issues from motorists saying that TV owners should be responsible for suppressing their TVs, not motorists their cars. The Transport Department had a cheap and easy solution to the problem – they disconnected the heaters! To be fair this was only a temporary solution and they did fit suppressors to all buses within a month.

In June EBCTD objected to Southdown's planned new circular route that was to go from the Archery via the town centre and Meads to Beachy Head; Mr Atherton said he intended applying to run the service himself.

In August the department issued a statement detailing cuts they were planning on making to the winter services. The usual array of letters appeared in the local press, with at least one calling for the sale of the buses to the highest bidder and another advocating Southdown could run a better service. Two factors were put forward for the decline in usage of the buses: televisions were becoming popular and people were staying in more to watch them rather than going out; and more people were buying small family cars and deserting the bus services.

Complaints about noise from the new buses were put to Cllr A. Neale, leader of the Transport Committee, who said that it was due to an exhaust brake and that previous buses were not

An AEC Regent V in a scene that is unrecognisable now. The green field behind is now a housing estate in Kings Drive. (Author's collection)

fitted with this device. This device eventually got disconnected on all the AECs and the braking system relied solely on the drum brakes.

In late 1956, during the Suez crisis, there was a fuel shortage and rationing was brought in as well as steep rises in prices. This affected Southdown and they cut evening services as well as increasing fares. Eastbourne managed to carry on without doing either, although the manager was given powers to cut services if the need arose. The inhabitants of Eastbourne were asked not to use the buses during peak hours when people were travelling to and from work. This would avert the need to duplicate services and thereby save fuel.

Permission was given to scrap the Leyland Titan No.1, bought in 1937, that had done over 683,000 miles. The manager was also told he could scrap the works Austin van that had started life as a car in 1935 and been converted into an ambulance during the war. Parts were difficult to source and the van was to be cut up and used as a source of spares for a similar van the department owned.

The Department's fleet of Morris vans in 1957. (Eastbourne Buses Ltd)

Southdown depot in Pevensey Road. The building still exists, although it is now a nightclub and the street is one way. (Author's collection)

1957

The annual accounts ending March 1957, showed a profit of £12,681 compared to a loss of £847 for the previous year. This was despite the problems with supply and cost of fuel. Permission was granted to buy a new LD01 Morris van. This would have a diesel engine and be fitted with fourteen seats so it could be used for staff transport, instead of a single-deck bus.

1958

The canopy constructed by the railway company at the station in 1932 originally had electric lights under it. These had been disconnected during the war and had never been reinstated. An inspection of the electric cables revealed that these needed replacing. Permission was granted to do this, and to reinstate the lights. Two signs that were suspended from the roof on the station concourse advertising the bus services had also been removed during the war and steps were taken to replace these.

Mr Atherton MD died in St Bartholomew's Hospital. He had been ill for six months and his deputy, Mr Cannon, had been filling in. He had been the manager for twenty years and was well liked and respected. His ashes were scattered at sea off Eastbourne. Conductors and drivers formed a guard of honour at his funeral service. Mr Cannon was promoted to Transport Manager in his place. His duties also included being Inspector of Hackney Carriages and Mechanically Driven Pleasure Boats.

On 25 August 1958 Eastbourne suffered its worst railway accident, when a steam-hauled express arriving from the North of England overran a red signal and collided with a twelve-coach commuter train that was just pulling away, pushing it back into the buffers. The bus depot received an emergency call for buses at 7.43a.m. and by 7.50a.m. the service was under way. Buses were supplied for the whole day while the wreckage was cleared. The department also supplied oxy-acetylene cutting equipment and lifting gears and, together with their staff, these were used to free trapped passengers.

Permission was granted for the Royal Mail to use single-deck buses for Christmas mail deliveries.

In December the Transport Manager reported that the Municipal Passenger Transport Department had joined forces with the Public Transport Authority and Passengers Vehicle Operators Association to form a Joint Fuel Tax Committee to initiate a campaign to try to bring pressure upon the Government to secure some relief from the very heavy taxation burden borne by the road passenger transport industry. The industry was taxed in three main areas: fuel duty, vehicle excise licence duty and public service vehicle licence duty. This amounted to 4*d* for every mile operated or 1*d* for every three passengers carried. This totalled £23,888 in the last financial year. The local council were encouraged to lobby Parliament and the Town Clerk was instructed to write to the town's MP Sir Charles Taylor.

1959

In January 1959 the Minister of Transport said that he would like the council to become involved in the Road Traffic Act 1956, which called for all vehicles over ten years old to be tested for roadworthiness, so the depot became an MOT test centre. Fees for the first tests were 15*s* for cars and 10*s* 6*d* for motorbikes.

The staff of the buses had enjoyed the privilege of having five free buses each year for staff outings. Staff were only allowed to go on one trip per year. A request was put forward that wives should be allowed to go on these staff outings. It was moved and seconded at a committee meeting that this request be denied. This was lost but it was decided to defer a decision until the next meeting. At this meeting a letter from the Union was read out stating that staff should be allowed to go on up to three trips each year and that they should be able to be accompanied by their wives. The committee decided that this arrangement should be tried out for that year only. These trips were run successfully and the arrangement continued in subsequent years.

In April, Mr Cannon addressed a meeting of the Holy Trinity Men's Society and although vehicle excise licence fees had been cut in the budget, making an annual saving of £2,500, he expressed his dismay at the Chancellor's refusal to cut the fuel tax bus companies paid. He said that fuel cost 3*s* 9*d* per gallon and 2*s* 6*d* of this was tax. He could remember when fuel cost 6*d* per gallon and drivers earned 5*d* per hour. Wages were now between 4*s* and 4*s* 10*d* per hour. Despite these increases the fares had hardly risen in fifty-five years, being only about 1*d* or 2*d* dearer now. Eastbourne was renowned across the country as the only bus company that had not increased its fares during the Suez Crisis. Patronage had increased over pre-war levels. He reiterated that the buses were out to provide a service rather than make a profit and over the years had contributed about £80,000 to the rate fund.

In August the Transport Manager apologised for issuing such a trivial notice to staff, but he had received a complaint from a member of the public that the pavement was being stained by crews throwing the dregs of their teacups onto the pavement and asked the crews to refrain from this practice!

Leyland Motors offered a Leyland Atlantean Hybridge bus for demonstration purposes for a week in November. There would not be a charge for the hire of the vehicle, but the undertaking would be obliged to bear the cost of comprehensive insurance and supply the fuel and crews. The offer was accepted. This Atlantean was the first front-entranced rear-engined bus to be used in Eastbourne.

Another offer of a demonstrator was accepted within four weeks. This came from ACV Southall and was for a Bridgemaster large capacity bus (seventy-six-seater). This was offered on the same terms as the Atlantean, except that it came with comprehensive insurance. Crews were given two days to familiarise themselves with the vehicles before they were put into service.

Chapter 7

The 1960s

More new buses; hovercraft service to Brighton; Diamond Jubilee; Leyland v. AEC; better working conditions; Lamb Inn accident

1960

In April a company called Eastbourne Coachways Services applied to the Traffic Commissioners to provide public transport services from the railway station to hotels near bus stops in Eastbourne. This was to pick up parties of pensioners who were coming to Eastbourne from Wales in July and August by train and transport them to their holiday accommodation. The Transport Manager objected to this and the Town Clerk was instructed to object to the Traffic Commissioners on his behalf. The Transport Manager was given authority to try to obtain this contract himself. He was successful in this.

In May a serious accident was averted by Driver J. Cooke. A mobile crane coming into Eastbourne from the west and down a long, steep hill descending from the South Downs suffered brake failure due to a hydraulic fluid leak. The driver of the crane had done well to avoid a collision when he came up behind the bus driven by 'Cookie'. He slowed his bus down and although the jib of the crane smashed through the upstairs rear window of the bus, he managed to use the brakes of the bus to bring both vehicles to a safe halt. An appreciation of thanks was conveyed to him from the Transport Committee and the Chief Constable.

A recruitment drive was initiated in April 1960. This was brought about by a shorter working week that the men won in wage negotiations. This brought the working week down from 44 to 42 hours a week, as well as increasing holiday entitlement to twenty-one days (including bank holidays). Average weekly wages were nearly £11 per week. These increases added £13,000 to the annual wage bill and the committee warned the public that this must lead to a fares increase. This would be the first rise since 1956.

When the proposed rise was put to the Traffic Commissioners for approval, they congratulated the Corporation for going so long without an increase, and for asking for such a modest increase in the face of fuel prices and wage increases. The increases were agreed.

Employing staff who already had PSV driving licences was becoming increasingly difficult, so the department set up their own driving school. To stop people learning to drive and then leaving to work for someone else, a contract was agreed where successful trainees would have to work a period of time before they could leave, or reimburse some of their training costs if they left early.

Towards the end of 1960, the committee decided to tender for five more buses with translucent roof panels, capable of sitting sixty passengers. These would have fleet numbers 56–60.

Eight companies were invited to tender for the bodies to fit onto the AEC chassis but only two did so, Metropolitan-Cammell-Weyman Ltd and East Lancashire Coach Builders Ltd. MCW Ltd quoted at £3,910 per vehicle, whereas East Lancs were nearly £1,000 cheaper at £2,988. East Lancs bodies weighed about half a ton less than MCW Ltd.

1961

In July the Transport Manager said he would need to order five more new buses in the very near future so they would be ready for the 1962 season. Due to the urgency it was decided that the chairman and deputy chairman would be able to decide on the successful tenders with the help of the Transport Manager. In August the manager submitted a confidential report to the council advising them why they had opted for five more AEC chassis rather than for slightly cheaper chassis from Leyland Motors Ltd. That report stayed confidential as far as I can gather.

In September tenders were invited for five more bodies to go on chassis already ordered. East Lancashire Coach Builders Ltd were again successful, fighting off close bids from Northern Counties and MCW Ltd.

The Joint Fuel Tax Committee had continued to put pressure on the Chancellor of the Exchequer to cut fuel tax duty for bus companies but with little success. In July, he increased the fuel tax duty from 2s 6d a gallon to 2s 9d a gallon. This would add over £2,000 to the department's expenses.

In November, permission was granted to the General Manager to tender for five more buses. Again tenders were to be invited from AEC and Leyland and the usual body-builders. These were to be delivered in 1963 and would be fleet numbers 66–70.

By June the five new AECs had arrived. Before No.57 was delivered it was entered into Blackburn Carnival by East Lancs and won 1st prize in its group (it makes you wonder what the other floats looked like!)

Other buses had come to the end of their useful life in Eastbourne. Three open-toppers, 6, 9 and 94, had been withdrawn from service. Most of the useful parts of No.6 had been removed and the hulk delivered to the Civil Defence for their training purposes. They were charged £25 for this.

Buses 13, 14 and 16 were due to be withdrawn and converted to open-toppers as staff time came available. When these were converted, three more of the older open-toppers would be withdrawn.

1962

A hovercraft service was envisaged by Southdown Motor Services as a rival to its own bus service between Eastbourne and Brighton. A Westland hovercraft arrived in Eastbourne to promote the proposed service that would cut the journey times between the two towns to 20 minutes. An application was made to the Air Transport Licensing Board for the necessary licences.

By July five new AEC Regent Vs (61–65) had arrived and been put into service. This allowed the Transport Manager to withdraw three of the eight Crossleys that had served the town since 1949.

Three more 1946 Leyland PD1s had been converted to open-toppers and these were to replace the ageing Leyland Titans bought in 1936.

An AEC in new white and blue livery in Lottbridge Drove. (Eastbourne Buses Ltd)

1963

At the start of 1963, the service ground to a halt with the worst snowstorms the town had seen since 1947. Parts of the town were without any bus services for many days. AEC Regent No.44 got stuck in a snowdrift on its way to Hampden Park and had to wait until a bulldozer could rescue it.

Mr Cannon, the manager, informed the committee that in April, the undertaking would be sixty years old and he had made plans to celebrate its Diamond Jubilee. He planned an official luncheon at the town's Congress Theatre. Those to be invited included the Transport Committee, those members of staff who had completed thirty years' service, local trade union officials, ten retired members, distinguished persons associated with public transport, both local and national, as well as members of the press. In a notice to staff attending the dinner from the manager, they were told that cocktails were available, but should anybody prefer a beer, they should ask the waiter. The same went for during the lunch when wine would be served. The notice then went on to say that he apologised for the fact they could not all be relieved from duty for the entire day and they should liaise with the inspectorate when they would be returning to work. Drinking and driving seemed to be condoned, but it certainly wouldn't happen these days. One hundred and twenty guests attended the lunch, yet only one of these was female, Cllr Mrs Lee. The staff were asked to make this lady feel 'at home'.

A brochure detailing the undertaking's history was published and commemorative badges presented to members of staff. One thousand commemorative brochures were ordered at a cost of £127. Two hundred badges were to be ordered at a cost of £54. An example of each was on display in the depot and staff were told they could have a complimentary brochure or badge, but not both.

AEC Regent MkIII No.47
opposite Eastbourne Station
in 1961. Judging by the lack
of traffic and passengers it
must be very early morning.
(Alan Hook)

The Transport Manager reported that there were ten members of staff that had completed forty-five years service and would normally be presented with a gold watch on their retirement. He asked for, and was granted, permission, to present these staff with their watches at this function.

The latest batch of five AEC Regent Vs (66–70), was delivered in May and June 1963. This meant that five old Crossleys could be offered for sale.

The Borough Surveyor and Transport Manager submitted a scheme for a new office block at Churchdale Road. This would be joined to the existing building and include lavatories and storage areas and release space for canteen facilities in the existing building. The estimated cost of this scheme would be £20,000. There would be additional parking spaces for over twenty buses behind this new block.

The Transport Manager said that in light of passenger numbers carried in the open-toppers, he felt there was only a need for five, not six, and had cancelled the conversion of bus No.15.

1964

At the start of the year, schemes to redevelop the centre of Eastbourne were put forward. One of the suggestions was to move the station further out of town and to use the present station site as a massive car park. Taking the buses out of Terminus Road was another idea put forward. Mr Cannon said that 8 million passengers a year alighted from the buses in Terminus Road and they did not wish to have to walk from a bus station to the shopping centre.

The contract with Setright for the hire of ninety-five ticket machines would end in June 1964. Discussions with Setright took place and they agreed that the useful life of the current machines was coming to an end. It was decided to extend this contract for a further twelve months, but a new contract for replacement machines for the 1965 summer season would be negotiated.

Buses were laid on in the evenings to take theatregoers home from their evening's entertainment. These buses would wait outside the theatres for the performances to end. For this special service, increased fares were charged – much to the annoyance of some ungrateful passengers! One of these ingrates refused to pay the increased fare. The committee asked the Town Clerk to prosecute the offender. This he did and the passenger was found guilty of breaking PSV Regulations (1936) and fined £3.

The annual accounts were submitted in April for the year 1963–4 and these showed a net loss of over £5,000, compared with a profit of £3,700 the previous year.

Two of the original batch of AEC Regent Vs beside an accident-damaged later model. Note that 50 and 51 are not identical. The radiator cap on 50 protrudes through the bonnet but the one on 51 is reached by lifting the bonnet. (Robin Bennett)

An AEC Renown demonstrator that could seat seventy-one was booked to come to Eastbourne in between 27 July and 4 August. This was a front-loading vehicle and the reason for booking this demonstrator was to ascertain the cost of operation and suitability for the roads in Eastbourne.

Mr Cannon informed the Town Clerk that he intended retiring on 31 March 1965 after forty-seven years' service with the Corporation. The committee placed on record their high appreciation of his services and decided to advertise for a new Transport Manager on a salary rising to £2,520 per annum. Twenty-two hopeful applicants applied for the post, but only two were invited for an interview – Mr R. Davies and Mr W. Holland. The Transport Committee, however, on considering the applications decided that Mr Holland need not be interviewed and that the post should be offered to the present Deputy Transport Manager, Mr Davies.

Due to the expansion of the town and improved services, it was decided that ninety-five ticket machines were not sufficient and 110 machines would be needed. It was also decided to purchase these outright at a cost of £6,220.

Work on the new office block started in September. This block was attached to the depot and the ground floor housed the reception and traffic office, while senior management had offices on the upper floor.

British Railways had started using the 24-hour clock when publishing timetables and the department followed suit in June.

The continued pressing of the Fuel Tax Committee was beginning to have an effect, as, in the budget, a further 6d per gallon had been added to the cost of petrol, but the Government wanted talks with the Passenger Transport Industry to relieve them of at least part of this extra cost.

1965

There had been no orders for buses to be delivered in 1964 or '65 so the Transport Manager proposed ten new buses be bought in 1966 and that the two major chassis manufacturers,

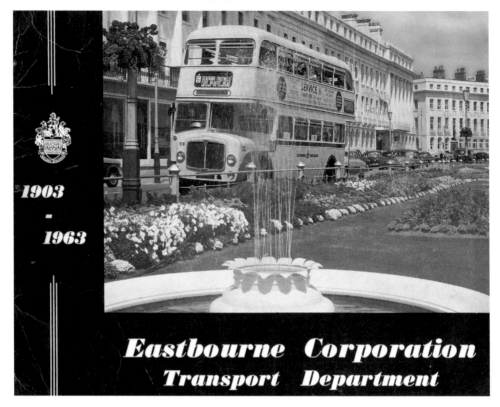

1903 - 1963

Eastbourne Corporation
Transport Department

Above: The brochure produced for the Golden Jubilee celebrations. (Eastbourne Buses Ltd)

Left: A sad sight in 1963 with two open-top Leyland Titans and three Crossleys lined up out of service awaiting disposal. (Robin Bennett)

A delivery of five more AEC Regent Vs (61–65) pose for the camera in 1962. (Eastbourne Buses Ltd)

AEC and Leyland, be invited to tender for these using the same specifications for chassis as the previous purchases, being rear entrance with radiators at the front. This time Leyland won the contract (Nos 71–80).

Later in the year the manager reported that there was now a twenty-month waiting list for new chassis and he recommended ordering five more double-deck chassis similar to those already on order to be delivered in May 1967 (81–85) and one single-deck one-man-operated bus. Permission was granted for the five doubles but the decision to purchase the single was deferred.

Concessionary fares were introduced under the Travel Concessions Act 1964. This Act meant that local authorities were able to make concessions for certain classes of passenger to obtain cheaper fares. These classes include men over sixty-five, women over sixty, persons under sixteen, students between sixteen and nineteen, blind and certain disabled persons. The Transport Manager told the committee that due to the high proportion of Eastbourne residents being pensioners, this would have a major impact on revenue, as well as putting a strain on administration to run the scheme. He would be submitting a detailed report on the implications of the scheme.

When he finally submitted his report in June, he said that giving pensioners half-price travel between 10a.m. and 4p.m. would cost the department about £18,500 in lost revenue, which they could not possibly hope to absorb.

Eastbourne Council discussed and approved the scheme by sixteen votes to twelve, and they agreed the sum of £18,000 would have to come from the general rate fund to finance the scheme.

The tenders from AEC and Leyland were received in February. Again Leyland chassis were about £300 cheaper per chassis. This time, however, the manager recommended buying Leyland, with vacuum rather than more costly air brakes. The usual body-builders of East Lancashire Coachbuilders Ltd, Metropolitan-Cammell-Weyman Ltd and Northern Counties Motor and Engineering Companies Ltd were invited to tender for supplying bodies for these chassis.

The Transport Manager put forward a report on the ancillary vehicles that were nearing the end of their working life. The 1957 fourteen-seater Morris van had now done over 90,000 miles and a Morris 5cwt van, HC 9544, had managed over 123,000 miles. The breakdown vehicle JK 5603 had been converted from a 1936 Leyland Titan in 1949 and had clocked up over 300,000 miles. He asked for permission to dispose of this breakdown lorry and to buy a Land Rover, which would be perfectly capable of towing buses. As both the breakdown lorry and 5cwt van were both in extremely poor condition, he was given authority to buy a Land Rover and a Morris 1000 van.

Drivers had their working week cut to 40 hours and would be earning a basic wage of £24 7s 9d per week while conductors would be on £23 9s. This increase would add a further £10,000 to the wages bill in a full year and the cut in hours with no loss of pay would mean a further increase of £8,000.

These increased costs, together with further costs incurred by fuel duty rises and predicted increases in mileage due to the town expanding, meant that fares would have to increase fairly dramatically.

The constant lobbying of Parliament by the Fuel Tax Committee paid dividends and the Government allowed transport companies to reclaim the last 6d per gallon that had been added to the cost of fuel in the budget.

The tenders for the bodies of the ten new buses were received and although East Lancs were about £60 more per body than MCW, their tender was accepted, albeit with another confidential report as to why. These two body-builders were the only ones that could deliver on time and were therefore the only two considered.

On Tuesday 22 June at 8.30a.m. the most spectacular accident in the history of Eastbourne Buses' history occurred. AEC Regent V fleet, No.66, was coming down the steep, narrow hill

AEC Renown Demonstrator opposite the depot and standing outside the original depot in Churchdale Road. (Eastbourne Buses Ltd)

from the Tally Ho public house towards the thirteenth-century Lamb Inn. At a slight bend in the road outside the entrance to St Mary's Church it clipped an empty Southdown coach going in the opposite direction. The driver lost control and hurtled towards the ancient pub. A baker's van was trying to pull out of a road adjacent to the pub. The bus hit the front of this van turning it over before slamming into the corner of the pub. Thankfully no one was killed in the accident but several people were badly injured.

About forty passengers, including schoolchildren, were on the bus. Two female and one male pedestrian were found underneath the van. Some passengers had to be cut from the wreckage. Both the driver and conductor were taken to hospital but were released later that day.

The driver's statement to the police reads as follows:

I live at 118 Pevensey Road, Eastbourne and am 31 years of age. I am a bus driver employed by Eastbourne Corporation Transport Department. I was first employed by the department three years ago. I went to South Africa and then returned to the department about a year ago. In my first tour of duty before going abroad I was a conductor. When I returned to the department about a year ago I started conducting again and then went through the department's driving school. I have been driving buses for about two months now. I have been driving cars for about three years. I hold a clean driving licence and have never been prosecuted.

On Tuesday, 22nd June 1965, I was driving bus No.66 on the journey from Central Avenue to Marsden Road, Langney. I left Central Avenue at about 8.15a.m. When I left the Tally Ho stop I had a fair load of passengers but the bus was not full and was not heavy. I drove away from the Tally Ho in second gear and remained in that gear because I saw a lorry coming up the hill towards me and about opposite the Cash Register premises. I flashed my headlights for the lorry driver to come on and he passed me on the hill. I went on and there was no traffic in front of me on my nearside. I changed up into third gear. As I passed St Mary's Church I was travelling at about 15mph. I was braking then and preparing to go into the stop at the Lamb Inn. I did not then notice any cars parked outside the shops on my offside. I saw a green

Southdown coach coming towards me and when the coach was beginning to pass the shops it swung out and then the driver must have seen me approaching and swerved back to the nearside towards the lay-by and the rear of the coach skidded out and struck my cab. The impact took the bus across the road and it hit the corner of the Lamb Inn. The steering wheel was spun so quickly by the impact that it burnt my shirt and scarred my chest.

At the time the road was wet but it was not raining sufficiently for me to use my windscreen wipers. The visibility was good. I cannot remember clearly if there was a motorcar parked on my nearside by the wall of the church but after the accident I remember seeing a red car, which had 'L' plates on it, parked by the church wall. I think the car was a Ford Anglia. Although my cab was badly damaged in the crash, I was able to climb out without assistance. I went round the back to help Conductor Taylor, as I could see that a number of the passengers had been injured. I think most of the passengers were able to get out of the bus without assistance, but one or two had to get off the bus by ambulance men. The police assisted with the taking of the names of witnesses as I was so shaken I found it difficult to write. A senior police officer, whose name I do not know, took the names of some of the witnesses. I heard a number of people at the scene saying it was not my fault. One boy was a passenger in the front seat, I don't know what deck, made a written statement saying the Southdown bus skidded across the road and hit my bus. I cannot say exactly how far the nearside of my bus was from the nearside pavement but normally I give plenty of room there between the nearside of the bus and the pavement. If the rear of the Southdown bus had not skidded out and into my bus I would have had plenty of room to pass safely. I think the rear of the coach skidded round about six feet so there was plenty of room between my cab and the cab of the coach. Definitely the rear of the coach skidded into me. The point of the collision was the front offside wheel arch. When I got out of the cab after the crash, the Southdown driver had moved

A typical view of the western end of Eastbourne's seafront looking towards Beachy Head. A Leyland Titan has the road almost to itself. (Eastbourne Buses Ltd)

the coach further up the hill and straightened it. I then saw the driver get out of his cab. I went to the coach driver and asked him what caused him to swing into me. He replied, 'What do you mean?' I am quite clear that there was no hazard at all in my approach to the Lamb Inn stop until the rear of the Southdown coach swung into the cab of my bus.

As I came down the hill the front of my bus was just about opposite the first shop when the coach swung to its nearside; this caused the rear of the coach to skid. The coach was never in the lay-by as it approached me, but the driver swung into the lay-by when he saw me coming. I cannot say if there were any vehicles parked to the coach's nearside. After the accident I did see a small motor invalid car parked between the confectioner's shop on the corner and the hairdresser's shop next door. The shops adjoin the lay-by. When I first saw the Southdown coach approaching it was about opposite the entrance to Borough Lane. I really cannot give an estimate of the speed of the coach as it came towards me.

I took the names of two witnesses, one was a boy, Burland, and the other was a Mrs White of 8 Marsden Road. She was waiting at the Lamb Inn bus stop. She said she saw the Southdown bus swerve into me. One of the police officers who attended the scene asked me what happened and I said the Southdown coach skidded and hit me. The point of impact was shown by a strip of metal on the front offside wheel of the bus, which dropped on to the road. The rear of the Southdown coach was some distance from the metal in the road after the impact and after the coach had been straightened up. I pointed this out to the police. There were no passengers on the Southdown coach and the driver was alone in the vehicle. I do not know his name. He seemed to be a middle-aged man. I did not see the baker's van in Ocklynge Road before the accident. It was not parked in that position as I came down the hill. Afterwards I saw it laying on its side in Ocklynge Road and up against the wall of the Lamb Inn. The van must have reached the junction just as the accident happened. If the baker's van had obstructed my view at all I should have seen it. I do not remember the bus hitting the baker's van. I think one of the passengers on the bus was an employee of the Southdown Company.

Witness statements varied enormously, with some saying that the Corporation bus was travelling too fast and others saying it was travelling at normal speed. Similar buses 67, 68 and 69 were driven down Chalk Pit Hill at full throttle in third gear to see what speeds could be reached but the maximum speed reached was 28mph due to the governor restricting the supply of fuel when the revs reached 1800 rpm. This dispelled some witness statements estimating the speed of the bus being between 35–40mph. It was clear, however, that there had been a car parked on the bus's nearside as it passed the church – it belonged to the vicar – and the bus had to overtake that as it made its way down the hill.

Two female pedestrians were standing on the pavement outside the Lamb Inn. They received serious injuries and were awarded £24,000 damages in the High Court, but had to wait until 1970 before these were agreed.

The driver of the Corporation bus was found guilty of driving without due care and attention and fined £20. He was never really happy driving buses again and returned to South Africa.

I remember I was a pupil at Eastbourne Grammar School at the time and a mate of mine, James, was on the bus behind which was held up, with the result he was late for school and was given detention. James was most indignant about this and said he was going to appeal to the master in charge of detention, who was a particularly feared German teacher by the name of Mr Morse. As James disappeared down the corridor in search of Mr Morse, my mates and I thought we'd never see him again! Imagine our surprise when James returned with a smile on his face saying his punishment had been cancelled. James went up in all our estimations and Mr Morse was never feared so much again as we realised he was human after all!

The bus, which was only about three years old, was back on the road by the end of the year. The chassis was repaired by the Transport Department and it had a complete new body attached to it. I drove this many times years later, but it was never right. The neck of the radiators on these buses protruded through the bodywork next to the bonnet. On this bus, when cornering, the radiator and bodywork would come into contact with each other making a loud grating noise. The workshops cut away part of the body to stop this happening, but no matter how much metal was cut away, the radiator and body still grated against each other. Eventually when the bus was taken out of service it was converted into a breakdown vehicle. It still exists and is now in private ownership.

In November the committee finally gave permission for the manager to tender for a single-deck, rear-engined bus. He stated that he would need one to replace the old No. 12, which was nearing the end of its useful life, as well as needing a single to assess the suitability of this type of bus on the streets of Eastbourne. He thought that he would need three new doubles in 1968 and eight more in 1970, but thought that it may be possible to have three of the latter eight as singles if the roads were suitable. Tenders for this single were to be invited from AEC, Leyland and Daimler.

Advertising contractors asked for permission to use high-quality paper for advertisements on the outside of buses. This was not agreed to, but adverts printed onto vinyl were accepted. This would reduce costs, but would signal an end to the sign-written adverts that had been skilfully painted directly on to the blue livery.

The Traffic Commissioners wrote to all operators in the area saying that they had noticed a rise in the number of complaints from passengers about late and cancelled services. It had been noted by them that it was difficult to employ and retain staff, but if the advertised services could not be adhered to, then cuts should be considered.

This page and overleaf: Pictures of the Lamb Inn crash. (Eastbourne Buses Ltd)

Chapter 8

The Advent of One-Man Buses

Daimler v. Leyland; industrial action; need for new depot; strike; profits turn to losses; Dial-a-Bus

1966

Tenders had been received for the supply of one single-deck bus. An AEC Swift was the cheapest at £2,889, the Leyland Panther was £3,072 and the Daimler Roadliner was the most expensive at £3,311. Mr Davies pointed out that the AEC's tender did not include a split braking system that would cost a further £25 and the Leyland did not include provision for air suspension at £239. He recommended that taking these costs into consideration, the Daimler Roadliner should be purchased as this had the added advantage of being the only one to which a body could be fitted that did not need any steps in the interior. His recommendation was accepted.

Although six body-builders were invited to tender for supplying the body, five declined and the only tender (£3,890) from East Lancashire Coachbuilders Ltd was accepted.

In March, the Transport Manager was told he could tender for three more double-deckers to be delivered in 1968. In April he reported back that Leyland could supply the chassis at a price £200 more than the five on order were costing and East Lancs had come back with a quote of 3 per cent more than the bodies currently being built. The manager recommended that these quotes be accepted and the committee agreed to this.

At the department's annual dinner, the Mayor addressed the staff and said she thought that single-deck one-man-operated vehicles were the way forward. This style of operation was already commonplace on the Continent.

Mr Davies, who had taken over as General Manager, did not share her view, however. In March he told a local reporter that one-man-operated vehicles would not have an impact in Eastbourne for some time, although he admitted that the Corporation had ordered one experimental bus, which would not be in service until May 1967 at the earliest. However, in May, the Chairman of the Transport Committee told the full council that if the experimental bus was a success, then more would be ordered. He added that there was not enough time for conductors to get in all the fares on the sixty-seat double-deckers. Although the council agreed to purchase one single-decker for £3,890, they also agreed to the purchase of three new double-deckers. This was eventually changed to five new doubles (81–85), which would be the last crew buses ever bought new for use in Eastbourne.

In June AEC offered a Swift for a week's free demonstration. This vehicle had a low front entrance and centre exit. Their offer was accepted.

The first of the Leyland PD2s. I had to include a photo of bus No.71, as it was the bus in which I learnt to drive and passed my test. (Robin Bennett)

Quotations for the purchase of six vehicles had been received. Wombwell Diesels Co. Ltd had offered £719 10s for fleet Nos 20, 21, 23, 28, 30 and 31. A Mr J. Wilson had offered £150 for No.29. All offers were accepted.

In July permission was given for the department to run a Town Tour service between July and September for the benefit of holidaymakers. There would be twelve trips daily between 10.00a.m. and 8.00p.m at a cost of 2s 6d per adult and 1s 3d for children.

The Transport Manager reported that the rules governing one-man operation had been changed by the Minister of Transport; the rule restricting this type of operation to single-deck vehicles had been lifted and this may well have a bearing on future bus purchases.

In November the Worthing Historical Commercial Vehicle Group had expressed interest in purchasing the Leyland Lion, fleet No.12, which was due to be taken out of service in May 1967. The group would be invited to make an offer in due course.

The manager also reported that Sweden would be converting to driving on the right in September 1967 and 1,200 second-hand buses with right-hand drive and doors on the left were being offered for sale by the Swedish government. The committee decided not to progress this offer.

The suppliers of the five double-deckers informed the council that the type of bus currently on order were becoming obsolete and they could change the order to front-entrance vehicles. The engine would still be at the front and the entrance would be via three steps through a door behind the front wheels. These buses could be supplied for an added cost of £400 each. Alternatively Atlanteans could be supplied with entrance door opposite the driver and only one entrance step. The cost of these would be an extra £1,300 each but costs could be reduced by £200 if translucent roofs and drop windows were not required. It was resolved that three Atlanteans with lower specification be ordered. The first batch of Leyland PD2s (71–75) was also delivered.

1967

In January, when the Atlantean demonstrator returned, the question was raised as to whether the department could finance five, instead of the three, Atlanteans on order. This would enable an entire route to be switched to one-man operation. The Borough Treasurer and Transport Manager were charged with producing a report on the matter.

The manager visited East Lancs body-builders to see the Daimler Roadliner, fleet No.86, being built. He had made some alterations to the specification and had fluorescent strip lights fitted rather than the tungsten lighting ordered.

The discussion on whether to increase the order of Atlanteans (87–89) continued. The Borough Treasurer thought it would be better to purchase two more single-deckers rather than Atlanteans as he wondered if it were feasible to one-man-operate a double-decker. Daimler had informed the depot that they could supply two more Daimler Roadliners by June 1968 (90–91). Two more Atlanteans (92–93) and two more Roadliners (94–95) were envisaged for June 1970.

Michelin contacted the depot and stated that they had developed a new X-type tyre, which gave better fuel consumption figures, and offered six sets to the department. The depot had a contract with the India Tyre and Rubber Co. Ltd to supply all their tyres. It was resolved to ask the latter company's permission to try the Michelin tyres. If they refused, the Town Clerk was given permission to terminate the contract with the India Tyre Co.

Five more Leyland PD2s (81–85) had been delivered, so the manager was given permission to dispose of buses 19, 22, 24, 25 and 40.

The Transport Minister was considering alterations to the limits that bus and coach drivers could work. They had not changed since they were introduced in 1930 and changes in traffic conditions meant that the rules should be reconsidered. The employers thought this may have considerable implications for them and was opposed by the Municipal Passenger Transport Organisation.

The manager asked the committee to allow him to fit electrically operated rear doors to some of the AEC Regent Vs. Cost of these doors would be £124 with similar costs for labour. This would not allow one-man operation, but would allow private hires without the need for a conductor. Permission was given to convert up to three buses.

In October, the Transport Manager reported that Leyland could supply three single-deck Panthers by June 1968 instead of the Atlanteans. The body-builders could supply single-deck bodies instead and this would mean a saving of £731 per vehicle. The Transport Manager recommended this alteration to the specifications and the committee agreed.

A Leyland Panther Cub was loaned to the undertaking in conjunction with the PTA's conference in September. The manager said that this bus would probably be offered for sale in 1968 and asked if he could ask Leyland for first refusal of this bus. He was told that in the light of the savings made by buying Panthers instead of Atlanteans, he could do this depending on the price being satisfactory. This price transpired to be £4,772 10s. As the price of a similar new vehicle would be about £6,500, this was deemed to be fair and the bus (No.92) was purchased.

In October the Trade Unions gave three months' notice to end their involvement in the National Joint Industrial Council for Road Passenger Transport Industry. The manager reported that from 9 November the local union had given him notice that they would be introducing a ban on overtime, standing passengers and non-co-operation in the implementation of one-man operation.

Of the ninety-two municipal operators in existence at the time, sixty-two had been approached by the unions for local negotiations and fifty had had action taken against them by the unions. The committee decided, though, that negotiations should still be done at national level and the local branch be informed that any agreement reached nationally would be implemented.

AEC Regent V fleet No.65 in original livery at the railway station. (Robin Bennett)

In December the bus crews took industrial action in pursuit of a wage claim. The local union wanted to return to local bargaining but the council wanted to keep to the system of national negotiations with the National Joint Industrial Council. This NJIC had broken down at national level, with the unions wishing to negotiate a new deal.

The 'work to rule' in Eastbourne meant crews would stop at all stops, the driver would select neutral and apply the handbrake, all passengers would be seated before the conductor rang the bell from the platform and a ban on standing passengers. All timing points were to be strictly adhered to. A ban on overtime was also introduced. These rules were designed by the local union and were not management or legal rules that should be adhered to. The crews also refused to overtake any bus that was in front of them. The department then refused to pay any bonuses that were usually earned by the crews and they would impose any deal that was negotiated nationally. This 'work to rule' continued for about four weeks.

The crews had an agreement that a bonus payment was made depending on the length of service. This was staged from 10s per week for six months' service up to 30s per week for twenty years' service. The Town Clerk said that this payment was dependant on staff working in accordance with the rules of the undertaking and by refusing to take standing passengers, they were in breach of this and should forego this bonus.

Back in London, the managements and unions had got back together and struck a deal that meant an increase of £1 per week for all adult staff. Part of the deal was that the old NJIC would be reconvened immediately. However, the Minister of Labour intervened saying that the settlement was against the Government's Prices and Incomes Policy and the company was advised it would be illegal to pay the increased wage.

1968

Five members of staff decided to sue the Corporation over non-payment of the wage award. They claimed the Corporation was in breach of contract as the increase was the result of negotiations between the NJIC and the employers. The Town Clerk informed the council that the Government had slapped a standstill order on the award and it would be illegal for the monies to be paid.

Union leaders advised the five busmen that their actions were unlikely to succeed, so they adjourned the summonses and by March the actions had been dropped altogether as the unions were assured that the rise would be backdated when the Government dropped their opposition to the rise.

One of the litigants went on to work his way up through the ranks via Inspector, Chief Inspector and Operations Manager, eventually becoming a director of the company in the 1990s.

Delivery of the Daimler Roadliners was expected by Easter and the three Panthers were behind schedule but delivery was still expected by June.

With these buses due to be delivered, the manager was given permission to dispose of the rest of the ageing open-top fleet. One of these went to Texas to create an 'atmosphere' at an English-style motel.

The one-man buses were used on the seafront and service 5, which ran from the town centre to Meads, started on 10 March 1968. The Meads residents lived up to their local reputation by moaning about these new buses. They called them cumbersome, noisy and accused them of emitting 'a vapour that is most unhealthy'. They also complained of the step being too high and getting wet while they queued to board while others paid their fares. Despite letters to the paper and the Transport Committee, economics won the day and the one-man buses stayed on the route.

By August the dispute over the £1 pay rise had still not been settled and the unions were threatening to strike. The unions asked for an assurance that the £1 wage rise would be backdated, but the Corporation was not able to give that assurance.

In September, the manager reported that the depot at Churchdale Road was no longer meeting the needs of the department. Extensive repairs were necessary, not least to the roof that would cost £12,000 to put right. The fuel storage tanks would soon need replacing and the whole depot needed rewiring, but fundamentally the depot had not been designed for vehicles that were 36ft long. The Borough Architect supported the Transport Manager's conclusion that it would not be possible to build new facilities on the existing site as it measured 6,100 square yards and a new depot was being built for a bus company of a similar size to Eastbourne and this was using 14,800 square yards. An estimated cost of a new depot would be £190,000, not including administrative offices, which would stay at their present location.

In September, the manager recommended that the livery of the fleet should be standardised and that adopting the white and blue livery used on the seafront services would allow easier spray painting of the fleet with a 5 per cent saving. The committee agreed with the manager.

He also said that he had delayed proposals for renewals until the Minister of Transport had published details of his Bus Grants Scheme. This had now been done and to qualify for a 25 per cent grant, the buses had to be used for stage carriage work and meet other conditions. These were not much different to the single-deckers they had purchased and the manager recommended the Corporation buy ten new single-deck one-man-operated buses. These would be used on the service 3 and Hampden Park routes. He was given permission to obtain quotes for the chassis from Leyland and Daimler and quotes for the bodies from seven body-builders – East Lancs, Duple, Marshalls of Cambridge, MCW, Park Royal, Northern Counties and Strachans.

A trial had been carried out using the Michelin X tyres and over an eleven-month period showed that increased fuel mileage was obtained amounting to about 5 per cent. This would mean a saving of £1,550 over the course of a complete year and the Town Clerk was instructed to terminate the contract with the India Tyre and Rubber Co. Ltd and to enter a new agreement with Michelin.

Parked behind the office block in Churchdale Road are, from left to right, Daimler Roadliner No.86, Leyland Panther No.8 and Panther Cub No.92. (Robin Bennett)

1969

Although it was normally the driver to fall foul of the law, in January 1969 two conductors were fined for failing to ensure the safety of their passengers – one for ringing the bell as a lady was boarding, the other for ringing the bus away as a lady was alighting. Both pleaded not guilty, but both lost, one being fined £3, the other £5.

The following month though, a driver of one of the new one-man buses was acquitted when he appeared in court due to an elderly lady falling from the rear doors as he pulled away. The police constable who took the statement from the driver went to the depot and sat in the driver's seat. He reported to the court that there was a blind spot in the mirror, where the driver could not see a young child or small adult.

Tenders were received for the bodies of the ten new buses. Seddons were cheapest at £3,500 each but the Transport Manager recommended East Lancs even though they were the most expensive at £4,390 each.

In April the Transport Manager submitted a report that any new garage should also include the administration offices. The Borough Surveyor put forward a plan showing possible sites for the new depot. The committee approved this alteration and adopted it as their new policy. These sites included Brampton Road Industrial Estate, the Gorringe Road area, the southern end of Lottbridge Drove and the land opposite the present depot owned by the Electricity Company and land at Churchdale Road set aside for allotments. The committee favoured the latter. A depot that would house eighty-four vehicles would cost £316,000 whereas one that housed sixty buses would cost £286,000. Again they favoured the latter.

The Road Safety Committee had expressed concern that the new single-deckers were not equipped with rear destination blinds and they thought these would be most beneficial to intending passengers. Mr Davies said that he thought that these could be a security risk as drivers would have to leave the takings unattended when they went to the rear of the bus. However he suggested that when the bus was on the same route all day, a card showing the route number could be placed in the rear window. A similar one could also be placed in the side window behind the door. His solution to the problem was accepted.

In September the manager recommended that the committee seek tenders for seven new double-deckers for delivery in the summer of 1972.

By November tenders had been received from British Leyland and Transport Vehicles (Daimler) Ltd for the supply of seven chassis. Bristol Commercial Vehicles Ltd declined the offer to tender. Both manufacturers tendered for 30ft and 33ft chassis. The committee decided that the Leyland 30ft chassis would be purchased at £25,635 each. The usual six body-builders were invited to tender for the bodies. Only two submitted tenders – East Lancs and Duples. East Lancs tendered for bodies with a combined entrance/exit and for separate ones whereas Duples only tendered for buses with a separate entrance and exit. The manager recommended purchasing vehicles with a combined entrance/exit and therefore East Lancs' tender of £6,337 per bus body was accepted.

Three of the AEC Regent Vs had had electric doors fitted. These were proving successful and the manager recommended that two more were converted.

1970

The arrival of the ten new Panthers was being delayed because of a twelve-week strike at Leyland and a serious fire at the workshops of East Lancs. It was anticipated that the buses would not arrive until October.

The safety of drivers operating one-man buses had been discussed and the provision of two-way radios had been proposed. Pye Telecommunications Systems had been approached for the provision of ten transmitter/receivers together with a control panel and aerial.

Eastbourne was expanding out of all recognition at the eastern end of the town with factories and large housing estates, both private and council, being built. Not a year went by without extensions to bus routes to these new areas. Link roads were also being built giving scope for varying routes into the town centre from some parts of town.

In June, the busmen held their first strike since the General Strike of 1926. They were unhappy over having to work summer schedules whilst a new productivity deal was worked out. The strike lasted two days. It started on Sunday 14 June. Over 100 busmen paraded through the town in uniform and with a loudspeaker van. They started at the depot and finished at the Town Hall. They waited outside the Town Hall while a delegation of nine union officials went inside to try to broker a deal. When they emerged they reported to their members that negotiations would start immediately and any deal worked out would be backdated. On a show of hands the men accepted this and voted to return to work.

The strike started a furious row between the local paper and the council. In an editorial, the paper accused the Corporation of refusing to get off its behind on the Sunday and 'snapping its fingers' at the general public. This was strenuously denied in an open letter released by the Town Clerk.

AEC Regent V passing St Mary's Church in Old Town at the spot where the collision with the Southdown occurred three years earlier. (Andrew Potts)

The scene outside the Martello Inn on Langney Rise, included as the landscape is as it was when I started on the buses, though it would be unrecognisable today. This was as far as the buses went. The area to the left of the photo is now covered by houses and a shopping centre. (Eastbourne Buses Ltd)

The 1939 Leyland Lion had been sold to the 'Eastbourne Lion Preservation Group' and they had asked if the Corporation could repaint the vehicle in its original livery in their workshops. This request was accepted.

By 1970 the finances of the department had taken a serious turn for the worse. Service cuts had been imposed for the summer services as a way of lessening the losses. Operating profits were down to just over £3,000 with mileage down nearly 29,000 and passenger numbers down 426,000 to 5,575,000.

By November a scheme to increase fares yet again was scrapped but replaced by another plan that would increase fares even more. An extra £25,000 had to be found to finance the pay award won by crews and mechanics.

A loss of £35,000 was predicted if measures were not taken. Letters from busmen who wished to remain anonymous appeared in the paper claiming the department had too many office staff, too many crews and saying that one-man-operated double-deckers was the way forward. Another correspondent also thought that not all pensioners should benefit from cheap fares. Many retired to Eastbourne and the first thing they did was apply for their concession card and thought that a period of residence should be completed first before being eligible for subsidised fares.

Delivery of the Panthers was furthered delayed because of a strike at Pilkington's Glass Company. The Transport Manager was given permission to dispose of ten double-deckers when the Panthers finally arrived.

The Eastbourne Region Preservation Group wrote to the Transport Manager requesting that they be allowed to purchase one of the AEC Regent Vs when they were withdrawn in early 1971 and in particular asked for first refusal on No.45 (AHC 445). Their request was granted.

1971

In January, the Borough Treasurer, Town Clerk and Transport Manager submitted a report which said that, owing to the ailing finances of the department, they should abandon the scheme for a new depot and concentrate on expanding the facilities at Churchdale Road. A decision on this report was deferred awaiting a report from all the Chief Officers concerned. This report was presented in April.

They presented three possibilities:

1 The construction of new workshops and offices with open plan parking at Lottbridge Drove for a net cost of £232,000 after allowing for the sale of the Churchdale Road depot.

2 Construction of a new workshop at Lottbridge Drove with the retention of the existing facilities at Churchdale Road for parking.

3 Repairing and improving the existing depot at Churchdale Road for £39,000.

The last option was chosen and recommended that work start as a matter of urgency.

On 21 February 1971 decimalisation took place, when the old £ s d were replaced with the current system. Rounding the fares up to the nearest new penny was calculated to bring in a further £9,000 in revenue. A bus had been parked in the town centre to give passengers a preview of the new coins to try to avoid some of the confusion and delays expected by the changeover.

In May the Transport Manager Mr Davies resigned to take up a post of Transport and General Manager at Doncaster Corporation. Eight candidates for his replacement were interviewed and Mr E.S. Leach was successful.

A system of Autofare payment system was tried on one bus from May. The driver carried a float and the passengers were to tender the exact fares. The scheme was intended to speed up

Unhappy busmen on picket duty outside the Churchdale Road depot during their two-day strike in June 1970. The two lads in the foreground and most of those in the background were still employed when the author started work there. The difference in architecture between the modern office block and original depot is apparent in this shot. (Eastbourne Buses Ltd)

loading of passengers. The equipment was fitted to the Atlanteans. One of these was parked in the town centre for a week so passengers could view the system.

The Deputy Transport Manager visited Kingston-upon-Hull, where Autofare was in use on all the buses and working very well. Loading times had been speeded up considerably. Change was not given, but passengers who had not tendered the exact fares were given vouchers, which could be exchanged for cash at the department's offices. The council in Eastbourne, however, decided by nineteen votes to ten that the drivers would carry change. Councillors called the voucher scheme 'utterly ludicrous', thought it most dishonest, and said that a driver could take someone's last 50p, refuse to give them change, then expect them to find some more money so they could take another bus to the depot so they could get their change back.

Some passengers tried to get the correct change before boarding by asking local shopkeepers for change. This led to complaints from them.

The fact that conductors would no longer be bagging up the money and paying it in meant that the safes with the fares in would be emptied at the end of the day and all the cash would have to be counted. A cash-counting machine was bought for £1,500.

In September the Transport Manager told the committee that there was still a waiting time of about two years for new buses and although the cost of bodies was stable, the cost of chassis was rising at about 1.25 per cent per month. There was another alternative to buying new one-man buses and that was to convert the Leyland PD2s to one-man operation. The cost of this conversion would amount to about £1,700 per bus. This compared to about £10,000 for new Atlanteans. East Lancs said that the conversions were mechanically possible and the unions had agreed to co-operate with assessing the potential of the prototype. Autofare would be fitted to the converted vehicles. He envisaged that all fifteen PD2s would be converted.

Before this could be done, the subsidies on new buses changed. The subsidy would now be 50 per cent instead of 25 per cent and the scheme would be extended another five years to 1980. This meant that the proposed savings made by converting buses rather than buying new ones was not so great and so the manager recommended that no conversions take place for the time being.

1972

The fare rises and cuts in services had had the desired effect, because in February it was announced that the department was back in the black and had made an operating profit of nearly £25,000.

The first of the Leyland Atlanteans were delivered in February. They were more complicated than previous buses and immediately caused problems for the workshop staff. In fact five of the seven new Atlanteans were blacked by the AUEW for two weeks before a peaceful solution was found. This solution guaranteed that fifty out of the fleet of fifty-five vehicles would be fit for service at any time.

A Mr Walter of Horam (about 15 miles north of Eastbourne) intimated that he would be applying to the Traffic Commissioners to run a rival bus service from the Archery to St Mary's Hospital in Old Town. The Transport Manager was authorised to oppose this and any other similar application.

An approach was made by an advertising agency that they would like to use the entire bus for advertising purposes. The committee inspected a bus in Brighton that already had an all-over advert on it. They were advised that the revenue from this sort of advertising could be as much as £1,500 per annum and that the cost of design and applying the advert would be borne by the advertiser as well as the cost of repainting the bus back into Corporation livery. There was some opposition to this at a council meeting with one Tory saying he thought the committee were putting gimmicks in front of Eastbourne's pride and traditional identity. He was in a very small minority and, again, financial considerations won the day.

A new form of public transport which was a cross between a bus and a taxi was being tried out in various parts of the country. This was known as Dial-A-Ride and the Ford Motor Company had offered a fifteen-seater radio-equipped minibus. If their offer was acceptable it would be for a seventeen-week trial period and operate in an area of Hampden Park not served by the present service. Formal objections were received from local taxi drivers, that this service would be impinging on their trade, and from Southdown Motor Services saying they thought the service should be restricted. The committee debated this and when it came to the vote it was deadlocked at three votes each. The chairman gave his deciding vote in favour of letting the trial continue.

It was decided to purchase eight more double-deckers capable of one-man operation (Nos 18–25) as well as a fifteen- or sixteen-seater vehicle to replace the 1950 AEC Regal.

Although the Autofare system started promisingly, by July the drivers had been experiencing problems. Because the committee had gone against the manager's wishes of not supplying change, the initial co-operation of the public having the correct fare had declined and now drivers had to carry a float of up to £40 to supply to passengers. This was having financial implications for the company as well as slowing down the boarding of passengers. A conductor was now on duty in the town centre whose role was simply to supply the correct change to passengers before they boarded the bus. Due to these operational difficulties the Transport Committee would recommend to the whole council to support a 'no change' policy.

At the Motor Show the manager had inspected a Seddon 'midibus' that would seat twenty-five to twenty-seven passengers and he recommended the purchase of this vehicle for £4,760 instead of the minibus previously agreed to.

In September a Leyland National was trialled. It met with rapturous comments from the management and drivers. It was equipped with a fully automatic gearbox and air suspension to give the passengers a very smooth ride. From management's point of view it could carry up to seventy-five passengers as against the fifty-eight the present singles could carry. The downside was that the earliest possible delivery date would be 1974.

The seventieth anniversary of the undertaking would be achieved in 1973 and talks had taken place between the Eastbourne Lion Group and the Eastbourne Preservation Group with a view to staging an exhibition, commissioning a historical film and tape of the depot and buses as well as producing a souvenir booklet. It was also decided that a better way of keeping the department's historical records should be found.

The 2 October 1972 was an epic day in the history of Eastbourne Buses – I started work there!

1973

By the start of 1973 the buses had again slipped into the red and were losing about £1,000 each week. They were stopped from increasing their fares by the Government's Prices and Incomes policy that had imposed a ninety-day freeze on all prices in an effort to curb inflation. This led to a record deficit of £33,000 for the financial year 1972–3. Since 1969 passenger journeys had dropped by 1,300,000 and miles run had fallen by 100,000. A loss of £52,000 was forecast for the following year.

In an editorial, the local paper predicted that there would no longer be buses running in Eastbourne by 1999.

A Leyland National about to start a journey to Rushlake Green. Note the running number 30 on the side. Although most bus companies use these as standard procedure, the practice was fairly short lived in Eastbourne. (Charlie Turton)

In June a Tory councillor suggested that a firm of consultants should be brought in to tackle the department's problems. He also thought that a merger should be sought with another local operator. His ideas were met with disapproval from councillors from his own party and were not acted upon.

Staff shortages meant that some services had to be cancelled. The Transport Committee approved the idea that to solve this crisis, they should start employing clippies. Clippies had been used during the war, but this would be the first time they would be employed under peacetime conditions. The first clippie to be employed was Mrs Carole Holiday.

The manager complained that the depot was no longer suitable for maintaining the fleet. The pits were not designed for modern-day buses. Only one pit was suitable for rear-engined buses so work was held up if more than one needed maintaining. It was a matter of urgency that new space was found to provide pits for these new vehicles.

In March, one of the Asians expelled from Uganda by Idi Amin started work as a bus conductor. He was a decent, likeable chap who was given a flat near the town centre. If we worked one of the rush hour extra buses, he would take his driver home for a cuppa. We were amazed at how well he was living. He had been given a grant by the Government of, I think, £300 plus another allowance for his two children. His flat was well furnished with a large TV. Before long he was driving to work in a car, while most of us were still cycling to work or having to come by bus. I remember a certain amount of resentment, none directed at him, but at the Government for their generous attitude.

On 12 April a seventieth anniversary run was made, following in the wheel tracks of the first ever bus service from the station to Meads. The 1950 AEC Regal was driven by the Mayor of Eastbourne who had taken lessons and passed his test first time especially for the occasion. Also invited to ride on the bus was a Mr Brockhurst, eighty-five, who rode to Meads on the first day of the service. The other passengers were long-serving members of staff, who between them had over 1,000 years of service to their credit. Anniversary 5p tickets were issued. One thousand of these were printed and the Transport Manager said they sold like wildfire.

Tenders had been received for eight new chassis and bodies (18–25). The usual combination of Leyland chassis with East Lancs bodies was chosen. They cost £12,800 each.

The Transport Manager told the committee that he wished to introduce an open-top service on the seafront and convert one of the existing fleet – either a single- or double-deck vehicle. His proposal received the approval of the Board.

Local taxi drivers appealed to the Traffic Commissioners over the proposals to run a Dial-A-Bus scheme. Despite their protestations, approval was given, although the service was curtailed because a Hail-A-Ride proposal was rejected. This was deemed to be unfair competition as it was illegal for a taxi to pick up more than one passenger who wanted differing destinations. Mr Leach told the commissioners that he wanted to start the service in September, but staffing shortages meant that this might have to be delayed until October. In fact it started in November, even though the department was desperately short of staff. The service did not do as well as envisaged and four weeks into the service it was losing £80 per week. The Swedes were contemplating a similar service and a Swedish TV crew came over and filmed the service.

In September, the headlines in the local paper read 'For Sale? Town Bus Fleet Shock'. The article went on to state that Town Hall officials were reluctant to discuss the talks and a top Southdown official refused to comment. Local councillors were very reluctant to talk to the press, but it finally emerged that on 20 August the Town Clerk had been approached by Southdown regarding the possible sale of the fleet to the National Bus Company. No conclusion was reached at this meeting.

The Liberals said they were against any proposed sale as they thought it was important to retain control over services in the town, but when challenged by a Labour councillor, they refused to give an assurance that they would not sell it.

On 3 October the council told Southdown that the undertaking was not for sale. No specific reason was given, but it was clear that the council wished to keep control over the bus services.

When the officers reported back to the Transport Committee they expanded on their decision. There were three reasons why they decided not to sell:

1   Although Southdown said they would run any service the council wanted, they would expect the council to underwrite any losses and the council would lose control over fares.
2   Southdown had no pension scheme for their staff. This would mean that all the staff that enjoyed being in the local government pension scheme would lose this benefit.
3   The County Borough Council was due to lose its status by 31 March 1974 when it was due to become a District Council and there would not be time to conclude the sale.

On 11 November the bus service was brought to a standstill when there was a lightning strike over the way a driver was spoken to by an inspector in front of the general public. A mass meeting was held in the Archery Tavern. A delegation then met the management, where differences were resolved and the buses then went back into service.

In November, one of the clippies passed her PSV driving test and became the first woman bus driver. Her name was Val Amman who had previously driven 3-ton trucks with the Women's Royal Army Corps.

In December, Eastbourne's first all-over-advert bus went into service. It was commissioned by a local travel agent and was covered in flags of different countries. It took the department's painter a month to finish the project. Advertising revenue from the bus amounted to £500 p.a. compared with about £100 for a normal bus.

Eastbourne's first all-over advert on Atlantean No.16 at the Ocklynge School turnaround in Old Town. (Phil Clarke)

1974

Despite making heavy losses, the three-month trial of the Dial-A-Ride service was extended for a further year.

A looming fuel crisis caused the Eastbourne Lion Preservation Group to call off the biggest-ever vehicle rally planned for the summer. They took the move before they had to outlay too much on organising the event. They had planned for over 400 vehicles to attend the event in Kings Drive.

Also in January, a driver was assaulted on a late night bus service in the Old Town area of the town. There had previously been trouble on this bus. To combat this, an extra member of staff 'rode shotgun' on this service to try to prevent any further incidents. One driver had a better idea – his wife would meet him before this trip and leave their Alsatian dog on the bus with him. This dog would sit at the front next to him for the entire trip. No bother was ever reported on his bus.

In June, the Transport Manager, Mr Leach, tendered his resignation. Four applications were received for the vacant position, including the successful one from Mr D. Sissons who was the Deputy Transport Manager. A Mr G. Livesay from Lancashire United Transport was employed as his deputy.

In the summer of 1974 the Transport Committee was merged with the Highways Committee to become the Highways and Transportation Committee.

The fares increase that had been imposed to deal with the expected deficit did not have the desired effect. The three-day week was held as being largely to blame for turning the expected trading surplus of £3,440 into a deficit of £5,285.

In 1968, section 36 of the Transport Act gave the council powers to run outside the borough boundary, providing the Secretary of State for the Environment was given notice. Although they had no proposals to run any such services, they did apply for powers to do so, as they thought they might operate some private hires and contract services outside the boundary if they had the spare capacity to do so.

1975

The eight Atlanteans ordered in 1973 (18–25) were expected to be delivered in March. The Transport Manager said that normally he would advise disposing of eight older buses, but in the circumstances, there was a national shortage of buses and it would be wiser to keep some of them for leasing to other operators. He was given permission to sell three in due course and lease the other five.

In May the Borough Officers presented a joint report to the Transport Committee concerning the replacement bus depot. There were still two main sites envisaged, one on the allotments at Northbourne Road and one on ground opposite the existing depot in Churchdale Road which was then owned by the Central Electricity Generating Board. The availability of this site was dependant on the CEGB's willingness to sell and the ability to find them alternative premises and this looked unlikely.

The Transport Manager pressed that the reasons for a new depot were as follows:

– The depot opened in 1910 and was extended in 1926.
– The Transport Committee were informed in 1966 that the depot was unsuitable.
– The 1926 workshops were constructed at a time when buses were 20ft long and 7ft 6in wide.
– The pits were designed for 20ft front-engined buses and any bus bought since 1966, except the Seddon, could not use these pits.
– Many of the vehicles had to be parked outside. To gain Government grants vehicles had to be at least 14ft 7in tall and the roof height in the main parking area ranged from 14ft 9in and 14ft 5in so for safety reasons Atlanteans were excluded.
– MOTs were carried out at the depot and new regulations were coming in during 1979 and items like roller brake testing machines could not be installed in the limited space available.

In July, the Traffic Commissioners granted that the Dial-A-Ride service could be extended into the new Hamlands Estate and more controversially that it could become a Hail-A-Ride service. East Sussex County Council were supporting the service financially, so this extension was granted to try to keep the cost to the ratepayer down.

In September the Transport Manager recommended that buses 53, 55 and 66 be disposed of. He informed the committee that owing to new regulations the Land Rover would no longer be suitable for towing buses and that 66 could be converted into a suitable breakdown vehicle for £500. Another municipal operator had approached him to see whether he would sell 53 or 55 for £250, excluding tyres. They would not be used for service work but used for charitable purposes. Both these schemes were agreed to.

In October an approach was made by an agent acting for London Transport and an AEC was sent to their Chiswick garage to see if it was suitable. The examination proved satisfactory and three buses were sent to a South London garage where they were based for service work.

Leyland Atlantean 21 still with trade plates in the windscreen soon after delivery to the Churchdale Road depot. Note the short-lived EBC logo on the side (Eastbourne Buses Ltd)

1976

At the start of 1976, pensioners in the town were up in arms. Firstly they were told they would have to pay 15p to cover administration costs when renewing their concession cards. Then they were told that their cheap travel would be confined to off-peak services. This was because the Government had called on the council to make savings of 7 per cent in their subsidies. This followed on from the local unions accusing councils in Sussex of being some of the meanest in the country when it came to subsidising public transport, which was vehemently denied by council officials.

The *Eastbourne Gazette* had printed articles calling for cutbacks and a halt for plans to build a new bus depot. The manager, Mr Sissons, invited the press to the depot to see the conditions for themselves. They then printed an editorial entitled 'Well. We were wrong'. It went on to say that they were amazed that the department was continuing to function in such run-down conditions with roofs leaking, lack of heating and chronic lack of space. They called the conditions diabolical and concluded that a new depot was needed urgently and it should go to the top of the list of the council's priorities.

The Dial-A-Bus service was being jeopardised by a row between two councils. It was still losing money and being subsidised at £4,000 per annum by East Sussex County Council, who wanted the Borough Council to put the fares up by about 30 per cent. The Highways and Transportation Committee decided to ignore their advice and go for a smaller increase and it was thought that the former council might withdraw their subsidy.

A local coach operator, Waterhouse Coaches, had applied to the Traffic Commissioners to run eight tours, but other operators including Southdown had objected. Their objection was upheld on the grounds that Southdown tours were under-patronised and there was not enough trade to warrant another operator. Waterhouse appealed the decision, but the Minister upheld the commissioner's decision. Ian Gow, MP for Eastbourne, said he would raise the subject in the House of Commons. He was concerned that a Government should protect a state-owned industry like Southdown against private competition. He thought the whole system of licensing should be scrapped and added that the idea that the Traffic Commissioner and Minister knew what was best for the general public was absurd.

Ted Waterhouse, the MD, threatened to take the dispute to the High Court. He held that Southdown were in breach of their licence because they picked up tour passengers in Eastbourne, but they only had a licence to run tours from Brighton and Portsmouth. Southdown countered that passengers boarding their coaches in Eastbourne were boarding 'feeder services' to Brighton and the actual tours did, in fact, start in Brighton. Waterhouse Coaches applied again for a licence to run these tours, but the commissioners said they would delay their decision until October and gave Southdown the green light to continue all of their tours during the summer.

Three days were set aside in July to hear evidence from both sides, but that proved not to be enough and the hearing was adjourned for two weeks.

Southdown got involved in another fight with Eastbourne Buses. The row centred on who was to provide services to and from Eastbourne's proposed new hospital which both operators could see as being very lucrative. Southdown diverted many of their services from using Willingdon Road to serve the hospital in Kings Drive. Doug Sissons pointed out that the hospital was on a loss-making route and he hoped that the increase in trade would turn this loss round. Whereas Eastbourne's buses were running commercially, many of Southdown's services passing the hospital en route to country destinations were already being subsidised by the County Council. On 23 June the commissioners gave Southdown temporary permission to serve the hospital. Before the commissioners could meet again to discuss the matter, the two bus operators had met to try to resolve their differences. Although they had not agreed on future services, they did agree to try to sort out their differences away from the commissioners and cancelled any further hearings by them on the subject. The row was solved by both parties agreeing who should serve new estates that were under construction. In July the full council gave Doug Sisssons permission to buy ten new double-deck one-man buses.

The loss-making Dial-A-Bus service ended in September.

In October a major new road opened in the town. Willingdon Drove linked the new estates at the eastern end of the town with the suburb of Hampden Park. If you look at a map of Eastbourne, you will see that the centre of the town is undeveloped and is destined to be a park, so the town lends itself for buses to go round the town in a circle. One service would go clockwise and one would go anti-clockwise. These services were well-liked by the public as you could get to virtually anywhere from anywhere within the town. The first service ran on Sunday 17 October with me driving it.

Three circular routes were introduced all serving different parts of the town. The town is just about the right size for one circular trip to be made in an hour, which made scheduling easy. All the routes had the same Achilles heel though – they had to cross the railway gates at Hampden Park and they are notorious for the amount of time they are closed. It was nothing for a bus to be held up for 15 minutes in busy times and there was not enough time in the schedules to catch up. The service became unreliable and finally led to the downfall of these very useful and well-patronised services.

One of the problems in the way of re-siting the new depot was lifted when Whitehall agreed that land being used for allotments could be used to build the depot and the council could acquire new land to move the allotments to.

In December, Southdown made public its proposals to shut its bus station in Pevensey Road and concentrate all its services at its depot at Susans Road.

1977

At the start of the year Southdown applied for planning permission to make £400,000 of improvements to their Susans Road depot, including new waiting rooms and a booking office. There were also plans to roof over the entire site.

In March, the Transport and Highways Committee did a complete U-turn on the proposed new bus depot as the cost had spiralled. Allotment holders, who had been told they would have to move, received the move with disbelief and cheers. Instead the committee decided to look at a warehouse site on an industrial estate at Birch Road. If the latter scheme went ahead it would mean a saving of £250,000.

In April, the AEC Regal was put up for sale. It was only used for the odd school run or private hire. It was hoped that a preservation society would buy it as it was in good condition and had only covered 170,000 miles. A Daimler Roadliner and an AEC Regent V were also put up for sale.

On 16 June the crews staged a lightning strike when the pay cheques did not turn up. The problem arose when there was an extra bank holiday to celebrate the Queen's Silver Jubilee and the office staff did not work on the Monday. This meant they were behind in their work. The crews were not made aware of this and many crews who were on rest days had come in to pick up their cheques and drivers with early finishes were kept hanging about with no news of their wages. Tempers boiled over and it was decided to hold an emergency union meeting and take all the services off the road so all members could attend. The buses were off the road for about 2 hours before the cheques arrived and the crews resumed services.

A row then erupted on whether the forty-five men who went on strike should be paid for the 2 hours they had withdrawn their labour. The Transport Committee and the Finance

Committee agreed that the money should be paid, but the full council overturned their decision and refused to pay it. The 130-strong union decided that if the money was not paid, they would start an overtime ban. At the eleventh hour, the ban was called off when the council convened another meeting to reconsider the issue. The NALGO union were unhappy, as they had worked about 74 hours between them to get the wages done and their request for overtime payments were turned down. At the reconvened meeting of the full council, they refused to amend their decision to pay the busmen. The union accepted the decision but claimed that it had done a lot of harm to the previous good industrial relations.

1978

This was the first year that Boxing Day services did not run. Doug Sissons, the manager, told the press that in previous years the services had been very poorly used and the council had lost money and very few other towns enjoy a service on that day.

In April the department celebrated its seventy-fifth anniversary. It celebrated in its usual way by copying its inaugural run from the station to the foot of Beachy Head via the seafront. Three buses made the run, the first being an open-topper which carried the Mayor and members of the council, the second carried retired members of staff and the third was a modern Atlantean which was open to the public. On arriving at Meads, the dignitaries were treated to light refreshments in the Pilot Inn before returning to the town centre. Souvenir reproductions of the original tickets were handed out en route.

In September, the costs of building the new depot had spiralled to over £1 million, over £200,000 more than the original estimate. The council decided to press on, hoping the Government would increase their grant towards the project.

A new 20 Centre Service was started for Christmas shoppers. This was a free service starting at a multi-storey car park and taking users to various parts of the town. It was free until January when a flat charge fare of 5p was levied. This was a 'bright idea' of a councillor but most of us at the depot thought it was doomed to failure as parking was free in Eastbourne and most of the roads this service covered was also covered by other routes. We were proved correct and the service was stopped a while later as it was a financial disaster, with the councillor who proposed it denying that it was his idea!

1979

In December, the police were involved in a high-speed chase that started about 10 miles east of Eastbourne. The vehicle being chased was a military Land Rover. A marked police car tried to stop the car as it entered Eastbourne, but it got rammed and could not continue the chase. Along the seafront another police car commandeered a Leyland Panther on the Service 3 complete with passengers and got the driver to swing the bus across the road completely blocking it. The Land Rover approached at high speed but mounted the pavement behind the bus and again evaded the law. The chase finally ended at the top of Beachy Head when the driver went off road and became bogged down. The driver gave himself up shortly afterwards and was taken to Eastbourne Police Station. After a cup of coffee to calm his nerves, the bus driver carried on!

There was a move to reintroduce workman's returns from the only Labour councillor on the council. This was defeated due to the inability of the ticket machines to issue returns and the pressure it would put on other fares to be raised to cover the revenue lost by selling these.

The new depot had been designed with two fuel tanks holding 8,000 gallons each. This was equivalent to about one month's supply, but to receive a whole tanker full of fuel, the stocks had to have dropped to under eighteen days' worth. Due to the uncertainty in supplies the manager asked for two more 8,000-gallon tanks to be installed so supplies could be guaranteed. These tanks would cost an estimated £10,000 to install. His request was accepted.

Two more designs for all-over bus adverts were accepted. These were for the Ship Inn in Meads and Sir Speedy Silencers.

Southdown asked for permission to use the Junction Road coach park rather than their depot in Cavendish Place as they were scaling down operations in the latter. Their request was accepted, provided they pay 50p for every coach using the facilities, which amounted to £3,025 for the first year.

The manager had received authorisation to buy ten new buses in the financial year 1980–1.

The manager stated that every new bus purchased since 1972 had been based on an Atlantean chassis, and although the earlier ones had proved to be reliable, the latter ones had not. The Ailsa was a front-engined chassis, which was not suitable for one-man operation, and the Atlantean chassis was supposed to be phased out from 1982. One had been on trial in the town and had proved to be most satisfactory.

The Dennis chassis were more expensive than the Leyland chassis by about £5,000 each and the Gardner engine fitted to the Dennis Dominator was about £1,000 dearer, but these engine/gearbox units were fitted with a retarder, which would save money in the long run as it would mean less wear and tear on the brakes.

The manager recommended that four buses from Hestair-Dennis be purchased (two short, 38 and 39, and two long, 40 and 41) as well as two Leyland Atlanteans (36 and 37). He also recommended that four more buses be bought in 1980–1 but a decision on which chassis these would be was deferred pending operating performances on the new vehicles. His recommendations were accepted.

The breakdown truck (formerly bus No.66 of Lamb Inn accident fame) about to tow in an Atlantean. (Robin Bennett)

Chapter 9

The Birch Road Era

Second-hand buses; moving to new premises; continuation of decline; expansion into coaching; use of consultants; Topline

1980

In February, the Transport Manager informed the council that the Government intended to phase out the grants given to councils who bought new buses. In the light of that, he was told to purchase second-hand vehicles and authorised to buy four buses at about £40,000 each, which was a quarter of the price of a new bus. He warned that, although this would be a short-term saving, it would lead to higher expenditure in the future for maintenance and repairs and as the buses were already halfway through their working life, replacements would be needed sooner. These were to be Leyland Atlanteans and were purchased from Ipswich Corporation.

In October, a new company, Vernon's Coaches, applied to run a bus service out of Eastbourne. They made a successful application to the Traffic Commissioners to run a service from Eastbourne town centre via Hailsham to the village of Cowbeech.

The 1980 Transport Act meant that restrictions on fares were removed. Mr Sissons told the Transport Committee that this could prove detrimental to the undertaking as other operators

Birch Road depot with a long-wheelbase Leyland Atlantean No.35 alongside one of the Atlanteans purchased from Ipswich Buses. (Charlie Turton)

Ready to be sold? A line-up of Leyland PD2s at Birch Road. (Robin Bennett)

could come in and cream off fares from profitable routes without cross-subsidising less profitable routes. This could mean that they may not be able to keep the less-used routes running.

The move to the new premises at Birch Road was undertaken in stages with the fleet still being stabled at Churchdale Road while only maintenance was carried out at the new premises.

1981

The department had been making losses for a number of years and the usual 'solution' of raising fares and cutting services had not improved the situation. A deficit of £400,000 was forecast and again the usual proposal to increase fares and cut services was put forward. This led to a response in the *Eastbourne Herald* from a mechanic employed at the depot who pointed out that no corresponding cuts in the top-heavy management had been made. He questioned whether a profit could ever be made when the department owned sixty-four buses but only had thirty-six on the road at any one time and this was during the peaks. He also questioned whether the department needed a manager, a deputy manager, two assistant managers, a technical assistant and a non-working foreman. He also pointed out that the amount of money the department had to pay towards the running of the Town Hall was higher than it used or needed. He pointed out that in July 1980 the staff had begged the Highways and Transport Committee to investigate the way the department was managed. He finished by asking when the top of the tree was going to be pruned as well as the bottom.

The department urgently needed new offices to be sited at the new Birch Road depot, but could not afford to finance them, so it was decided to use £247,000 that the department had been granted to purchase new buses to build offices instead. The Transport Manager and Borough Treasurer said that the council were free to spend its bus purchase grant in any way it wanted. Meanwhile the old depot at Churchdale Road was on the market for £250,000.

The last AEC Regent V was withdrawn from service in August 1981. To commemorate this the staff were allowed to take Bus 56 out on a last run. It was taken to the town of Rye and those on board went on a tour of the town's numerous hostelries. Those wishing to, took turns in driving on the way there, and as I was the only one who managed to stay sober, drove it home again. The special headboard was made up in the company's workshops.

Eastbourne Buses' first two coaches, Leyland Leopards 90 and 91, pictured at Birch Road in 1986. (Robin Bennett)

1982

1982 saw the introduction of coaches to the fleet of Eastbourne Buses with the purchase of two coaches. These were fifty-three-seat Leyland Leopards, purchased second-hand. Five more Dennis Dominators (42–46) were also delivered.

The crews of the buses had for some years used a Christmas club that was run by one of the conductors. On the day of the proposed payout in December, the conductor administering it phoned in sick. The conductor in question had been going out for the last few weeks with a young lady with expensive tastes and the men's fears were confirmed when the conductor was arrested. The police released a statement saying that up to £3,000 was missing from the fund.

In March 1983, he was charged with stealing £1,650 and released on police bail. When his case finally came up at Lewes Crown Court in July, he was found guilty and was given a nine-month prison sentence, suspended for two years with a two-year supervision order. Needless to say he lost his job on the buses. His family had a whip-round and most of the monies were eventually paid out to the club members.

The summer seasons in Eastbourne had been a problem for a number of years due to the influx of thousands of foreign students swamping the town. They travel to colleges and schools during the rush hour and services could not cope with their numbers and regular passengers were often left behind, causing complaints and antagonism. Headlines in the local paper in July read 'Blunder-Buses'. A shortage of drivers did not help the situation, and neither did the fact that

One of the first batch of Dennis Dominators approaching the town centre. This one was painted in an all-over advert for a local furnishers. (Charlie Turton)

three buses had been hired out to other operators. Management defended this decision by saying it was pointless keeping the buses if they had no drivers. The overcrowding was compounded as there was also a rail strike, making this possibly the worst year for overcrowding on record.

1983

In February, the council decided to employ a firm of consultants to sort out the department's financial problems. A group of three councillors, one from each party, was to choose the successful company from a shortlist of three, but the Labour councillor, Roland Hutchinson, resigned from the panel as one of the three was Travers Morgan Planning, who had a senior partner who was involved in the Serpell report into British Rail which suggested extreme cutbacks in their operations and services.

The Borough Council were prepared to pay £30,000 on a study, of which they hoped East Sussex County Council would pay £15,000. Colin Buchanan and Partners were eventually awarded the contract. They said they would be conducting door-to-door surveys as well as interviewing people at hospitals and schools to ascertain what the public wanted from their bus service. They would also be looking at maintenance of the fleet, timetables and management procedures to try to curb rising costs. The study was expected to last six months.

In March, the local paper headlined an article that Buchanan's had been employed by three other south coast towns and this has led to the loss of hundreds of jobs. The towns involved were Plymouth, Portsmouth and Southampton and 324 jobs were lost in total.

In Portsmouth there was a public outcry when a part of the town was left without any service, there were long queues for buses as too many staff were laid off and then more had to be recruited to take their place and their report had made no difference to the losses they were making.

In Plymouth, 180 jobs were lost and passenger levels were down 5 per cent.

In April the department celebrated its eightieth birthday by operating an anniversary run commemorating the original journey from the town centre to Meads. A preserved AEC Regent V owned by a member of staff was used to transport the dignitaries. The public enjoyed a free trip on a special bus that followed and a free town tour lasting 90 minutes. Commemorative tickets were issued for these trips. Photos from the department's archives were on display at the Pilot Inn at Meads as well as a small display of buses in the pub's car park. The licensee of the Pilot at the time was an ex-Eastbourne bus driver.

Later on in the year a free vintage bus service was operated along the seafront for enthusiasts and public alike. This service was run by old Eastbourne buses, the oldest being a 1936 Leyland TD4 and the newest a 1966 AEC. Ten thousand passengers were carried.

In April, at the new depot, a bus that was being driven on to a set of ramps overshot and rolled off the end. A cleaner who was standing in front of the bus just managed to jump clear as the bus crashed into some staff lockers before demolishing a wall. The bus suffered damage to its front panels and windscreen, but luckily no one was injured. Meanwhile the old depot at Churchdale Road was being vandalised and a building firm had been given permission to use it.

By November Buchanan's were making public some of the findings in their report. These included that about 37 per cent of passengers thought the crews were rude and unhelpful. Passengers in Eastbourne also took longer boarding on average. This was due to the fact that much of the population was elderly and that the fares were complicated, with more than average requiring change.

Both Doug Sissons and his deputy George Livesay applied for early retirement. Whether this was prompted or not by the findings of the Buchanan report was not made public. They agreed to stay on until replacements could be found.

The report's findings prompted an outcry from the public and staff alike. Buchanan's found it difficult putting things into plain language – using the phrase 'slight disbenefit' where they meant up to 50 per cent of some services would be scrapped. They recommended converting some routes to one-man operation, although this would make the service unreliable. It was also proposed to make thirteen drivers and all conductors redundant. They also recommended buying more second-hand buses. Letters appeared in the local paper proclaiming they would be second-hand buses for a second-class service.

Three second-hand buses had been bought from Southampton nine months previously and they had still not been put into service. They were already fifteen years old. Management said that they needed mechanical work doing to them and repainting into Eastbourne's livery. They went on to say that the important thing was that they would be on the road by next summer! The union pointed out that this was clearly nonsensical.

These ex-Southampton buses were semi-automatics with an electrically operated gearbox. They had a very simple but effective way of making sure the buses could not be driven with the doors open – on the gear selector control, where fifth gear would normally be, was the position for opening the doors. This is fine if you have a fleet of buses like this, but we only had three, which we rarely drove. The problem was that most drivers were in the habit of selecting the gear to pull away while the last passenger or two were alighting, ready for a quick getaway.

Two styles of Leyland Atlantean parked at the rear of the depot at Churchdale Road. No.11 had a gearbox operated by compressed air and No.21 an electric box. (Author's collection)

An ex-Southampton Transport Atlantean in experimental livery. (Robin Bennett)

With these buses, this meant when the gear was selected, the gear lever was taken from the 'doors open' position and these buses were responsible for more passengers being trapped in the doors than the rest of the fleet put together!

The union's campaign against the Buchanan Report was proving to be effective as after a meeting lasting three-and-a-half hours with the council, an announcement was made saying the cuts would not go ahead. An editorial in the *Eastbourne Gazette* heaped praise upon the union over the way they were conducting the fight against Buchanan's and urged the public to give them their backing.

1984

The council set up a Steering Committee to examine Buchanan's proposals in detail and the council amazingly decided to pay Buchanan's another £12,500 to help implement their plans. £1,790 of this was to pay for publicity and passenger information, £2,047 for drawing office staff and £3,186 for general advice. Buchanan's came up with statistics stating that passengers who bought a weekly season ticket for £6 only used them six times each week. As the maximum fare was only 60p, this meant that the average season-ticket user was losing £2.40 each week. Figures like this helped bring their report into disrepute.

In March, the new Transport Manager was named as Mr Roger Bowker. The new service started in May and was chaotic. Passengers had no idea where the new services were going and this led to friction between them and the crews. Extra buses had to be laid on because the service could not cope with the demand. Fares had changed from a stage system to a zonal system and this led to more confusion. And to cap it all, the new manager proposed changing the livery to an awful primrose and brown. A bus painted in this new livery was parked in the town centre as a mobile information point and public reaction to it was not complimentary.

Most of the changes proposed by Buchanan's were abandoned, either sooner or later. In June an all-party committee was set up to look into the report with one councillor calling it 'one of the town's biggest follies'. This led to the council labelling the report 'misleading and inefficient' and the Chairman of the Highways and Transport Committee apologised saying that Buchanan's had 'failed miserably'.

The debate on the proposed new livery rumbled on and in September four buses in different liveries were parked in the town centre and the public were able to fill in forms to say which scheme they preferred. A variation on the traditional blue and cream livery came out on top with primrose and brown trailing badly in last place.

By October, privatisation was rearing its ugly head. A novel scheme was put forward from the Transport Manager, Roger Bowker, and the Chairman of the Highways and Transport Committee to thwart this – ban buses and introduce trolleybuses! They visited the Birmingham Motor Show and examined the chassis of one such vehicle being built by GEC and Dennis. Although there were advantages in fuel costs and being kinder to the environment, capital costs were against them with a trolleybus costing about £100,000. If the scheme were to go ahead, then petrol- and diesel-engined buses would be banned from the town centre, thus doing away with any competition.

1985

In March, the Secretary of State for Transport, Nicholas Ridley, visited Eastbourne to try to allay fears over his White Paper that proposed putting bus services out to tender. These were to be included in the 1985 Transport Bill, which was to drastically change the way buses were operated in this country. Mr Ridley spoke to management and staff at the Birch Road depot before being taken by bus to the Town Hall, where he spoke to officials. At a press conference afterwards, he said his Bill was designed to open up services for the benefit of passengers and cut the amount of subsidies granted by councils. Under the Act, councils would still be able to subsidise unprofitable services, but these would have to be put out to tender and they would have to accept bids from private operators if their bids offered the best value for money. He maintained safety standards would not deteriorate and regular safety checks would take place.

The local council remained unconvinced. So did the busmen. Thirty-two of them, together with local cab drivers, joined bus drivers and cabmen from around the country in a protest in London. They took with them a petition of 6,500 signatures.

A strike was called by the TGWU over the issue of pensions in the Transport Bill. This was to be held on 29 October. The local authority climbed down and allowed the employees of what was to become Eastbourne Buses Ltd to stay in the East Sussex County Council final salary scheme.

On a brighter note, a new open-topped bus was unveiled. It was one of two that had been converted from the Atlanteans purchased from Ipswich Corporation. The cost of the conversion had been subsidised by the Eastbourne Hotels Association. One was painted blue and called the Eastbourne King, the other red and called the Eastbourne Queen. A few drivers objected to sitting behind a sign that said 'Eastbourne Queen'!

Two luxury seventy-seat double-deck coaches were purchased to add to the coaching fleet. They were to be numbered 1 and 2. They were used for private hires as well as excursions. Eastbourne Coaches made their first trip to mainland Europe in July when they took Eastbourne Silver Band to Fecamp, near Dieppe, to take part in an annual festival Fête de la Mer.

London Liners in both liveries at Battersea. (Robin Bennett)

One of the Dodge minibuses purchased for the Red Carpet Service. (Robin Bennett)

By December, plans were being readied to register the Transport Department as a private company to comply with the new Act. It was to be called Eastbourne Buses Ltd. The Board was to be made of two working directors and four councillors, two Liberals and two Tories. The Chairman of the Board would be a councillor of the ruling party.

1986

The two double-deck coaches purchased the previous year were used on a new service run in conjunction with London Transport: the 'London Liner'. A bus left Eastbourne in the morning and operated a return service in the afternoon whilst a London Transport bus came from London in the morning and returned in the afternoon. The service started on 17 May and ran until the end of September. The route was via Crowborough, Tonbridge and Bromley. Although the service from London arrived in Eastbourne with fairly good passenger numbers, the service to London was never well-patronised and the service was soon withdrawn.

Dodge midibuses were introduced on some routes from 26 October owing to the non-viability of running double-deckers. Roger Bowker was very keen on presenting a good image and marketed these as the 'Red Carpet Service'. Volunteer drivers were hand-picked based on appearance and passengers could be picked up at or near their homes on some estates. A slightly higher fare was charged for this service. The service did not get off to a brilliant start as all the midibuses ran out of fuel about 4p.m, as their fuel tanks were not big enough to do a whole day's work. This meant that schedules had to be rearranged so that they could return to the depot to be refuelled.

Another Volvo coach, costing £61,000, was delivered in March. This was numbered 3 in the coaching fleet.

More minibuses hit the streets of Eastbourne when Southdown bought a fleet of Mercedes for their local services. They received a mixed reception from the public with the main complaint being lack of space on board. These minibuses mainly served Polegate, but service 43 to Hamlands estate was introduced, which was seen as direct competition to the town's service 19.

The Transport Act 1985 was enacted on 26 October and Eastbourne Buses Ltd came into being with all the shares owned by Eastbourne Borough Council. This allowed the company

Two Daimler Roadliners, 86 and 90, at the rear of the Churchdale Road depot. They could normally be seen here as they were so unreliable and disliked by crews. They were mainly used on peak time services. (Robin Bennett)

to compete for tenders and operate outside the borough. Services were soon running through Hailsham to Uckfield and services could finally run to the top of Beachy Head after years of frustration at having to terminate at the foot. The downside of the Act was that Southdown and any new operator could now compete on an even footing within the boundary.

Eastbourne Buses bought out the small firm of Vernon's. The purchase consisted of a Leyland Leopard and the route to Rushlake Green.

1987

Eastbourne Buses Ltd joined forces with Southdown and set up a company called Topline to attack Hastings & District on its own territory in Hastings. Eastbourne owned 49 per cent and Southdown 51 per cent. Originally Brighton and Hove Buses were to be part of the new company but decided against it.

Complaints were received from the crews and public in Eastbourne that the fleet's better vehicles had been transferred to Topline leaving the older, less reliable buses to keep the service running in Eastbourne.

Topline's buses were painted in a striking black and yellow livery. The services started in May. Originally the buses operating these services were stabled in Eastbourne, but the dead mileage

Twelve new Leyland Olympians lined up on a Sunday morning outside the depot for the official handing-over ceremony. (Eastbourne Buses Ltd)

to Hastings was costing £720 per week in diesel so a site to stable the buses in Hastings was sought and staff would travel to and fro in one bus. Eventually the staff clocked on and off at the new site in Hastings.

Hastings & District had a bad reputation for reliability and Topline successfully tendered for some schoolwork even though their tenders were higher than Hastings & District. They then registered some routes to run commercially between school trips. H&D's unreliability stemmed from a decision to run minibuses on a more frequent headway, but they could not subsequently employ enough drivers to operate the improved services. The South Eastern Traffic Commissioners banned them from registering any more routes, but the Transport Tribunal subsequently overturned this decision

Back in Eastbourne six ex-London Transport Leyland Nationals were purchased and four minibuses were swapped for four Atlanteans from Ipswich Corporation.

1988

Twelve Leyland Olympian (47–58) buses were lease-purchased. An official handover was organised with all twelve vehicles lined up in an arc outside the workshops at Birch Road. Dignitaries from the council, manufacturers, etc. were all invited to the ceremony. A buffet was laid on inside the works. What the official photos do not show is that the buses had already been in service. One of them had been hit in the rear by a dustcart a couple of days before the ceremony and repairs could not be done in time. When the party went inside for drinks and food the crumpled rear of this bus was clearly visible through one of the depot windows.

Roger Bowker MD left the company to take up a new post with Stagecoach in London. His place was taken by David Howard, who was to become a very popular manager with the staff, if not with local councillors, as he tried to run the concern more as a business rather than a social service!

1989

In March Hastings & District retaliated against Topline by introducing their 'Eastbourne & District' minibuses. They ran over Eastbourne's busiest corridor between Hamlands and Shinewater. They ran free for the first week.

Topline made a loss of about £338,000 in the first two years of operation. In September, Eastbourne sold its share in Topline to Southdown for a nominal amount. Southdown entered into negotiations with Generalouter, the holding company of Milton Keynes Citybus, which was also in talks to buy Formia, the holding company for H&D. When Stagecoach heard that these talks were foundering, they made an offer to buy Formia, which had been set up by three senior managers of H&D, to buy the share capital of H&D from National Bus Company. H&D had been established as a separate subsidiary from NBC in 1983.

Topline's services were merged with H&D services. After the takeover their small depot closed with the buses being transferred to the St Leonards depot. The new combined service ran under the name of Hastings Buses.

The Corporation were considering a sell-out to the staff of Eastbourne Buses, not that the staff were greatly aware of this. Other companies that had been the subject of staff buyouts in the area had subsequently been sold to Stagecoach and they had confirmed they would be interested in acquiring Eastbourne Buses if the offer came their way.

Chapter 10

The 1990s

Monopolies and Mergers investigation; agreements with Romney, Hythe and Dymchurch Railway; Eastbourne Buses Ltd for sale

1990

On 29 May 1990, the Monopolies and Mergers Commission investigated the acquisition by Stagecoach (Holdings) Ltd (Stagecoach) of Formia Ltd, which was the holding company for Hastings & District. Companies were not allowed to supply over 25 per cent of local services in a substantial part of the UK. In this case the area in question was most of Sussex and Kent. There were no other major operators located close to Hastings or Bexhill, which are surrounded by rural areas with few commercial services. In this case, they did not believe that competition from other operators or potential competition from new entrants would be sufficient to offset the loss of competition in the Hastings or Bexhill areas, but there would remain a degree of competition between Southdown and Eastbourne Buses Ltd in Eastbourne. In their view, the creation of a dominant position in Hastings and Bexhill removed a main constraint on the fares and tender prices that could be charged, and the main stimulus to efficiency and to the improvement of services, and may have been expected to lead to higher fares and tender prices and to lower standards, quality and frequency of service and less choice. They were also concerned that the strengthening of Stagecoach's position could weaken other operators, and they could, by future acquisitions, increase their dominance further. They therefore concluded that the merger may be expected to operate against the public interest, but they stopped short of making Stagecoach sell Hastings & District. They thought that divestment would be likely to mean that, in this limited area, if the existing dominant supplier merely gave way to another, this would risk disruption of services and inconvenience to passengers while the change was being effected.

They did, however, recommend a number of measures to improve local accountability, to prevent short-term retaliation against new entrants, to notify further acquisitions, and to limit the cost of tenders. They believed that these measures would be more effective than divestment in remedying the adverse effects of the merger.

1991

Proposals to purchase two new Leyland Javelins (23, 24) and two fairly new second-hand vehicles (25, 26) had to be rethought due to cash-flow problems. These would now have to be lease-purchased. A policy of purchasing single-deck buses was being pursued due to the price of double-deckers.

The MD reported that no new buses had been purchased between 1982 and 1988 and, although some second-hand buses had been purchased to eliminate the dual-door vehicles from the fleet, the present fleet was becoming increasingly difficult to maintain and some mileage had been lost due to lack of available vehicles. Ideally four buses would be replaced every year, but finances would not allow this.

The MD informed the Board that Stagecoach had taken over Southdown Motor Services Ltd and subsequently Hastings & District Ltd and Eastbourne Buses' share of Hastings Topline Buses Ltd.

They had also been behaving aggressively in Eastbourne by running services to Shinewater and Hamlands estates and had shown a desire to encroach on other services. Mr Howard said if that was the case, then Eastbourne Buses would retaliate. The MD of Southdown approached Mr Howard with a view to reducing competition so both operators would benefit. Ticket inter-availability and the possibility of Eastbourne Buses maintaining Southdown's fleet were looked at.

1992

Although there had been nothing in the Queen's Speech about the sale of Municipal Bus Companies, at the time it was thought that divestment would still be required within the lifetime of the Government. Eastbourne was one of only three Municipal Companies that had not looked into ESOP/MEBO (Employee Share Ownership Plan/Management Employee Buy Out). A report by the Executive Directors to the Board was presented on the possible sale of the bus company. They reported that the Government had a timetable for the sale of all Municipal Bus Companies, but a voluntary sale could be considered. The Government's timetable was to have a Bill presented to Parliament by November 1993, to receive Royal Assent by September 1994 and to start the sales by January 1995.

Although the company would have to be sold by competitive tender, the Secretary of State has shown no encouragement for direct sales, except for management staff buyouts, which he supported with an allowed discount of up to 5 per cent, with local councils being able to assist by financing legal costs. Local authorities were given the power to exclude any purchasers that would create a monopoly. In Eastbourne's case, this would include Stagecoach Holdings, but it was thought that they might start predatory services that may make any proposed staff buyout very difficult, if not impossible. This had been done in Maidstone, leaving the council with a liability rather than an asset, so it was vital there was no public discussion on the subject. Stagecoach had been stockpiling vehicles in the area, so competition was highly likely.

The unions were asked if they wished to participate in further information-gathering without commitment to further action, but they declined. The directors had a preliminary meeting with financial advisers as well as meetings with other directors of bus companies in similar positions.

The directors concluded that they did not want to initiate buyout proceedings, but should the council decide to sell they would consider making an offer, providing the council agreed to authorise the expenditure of up to £15,000 on a feasibility study into the market value of the company, the likelihood of finance for a buyout being available, staff pensions and contracts and directors' contracts. They also pushed for a confidential meeting between Board and Shareholders, but stressed that they thought that it was not the right time for a buyout.

Dennis Lance No.14 enters the bus precinct on a glorious summer's day. Note the number plate that bore David Howard's initials. Many drivers accused him of wasting money in buying this. (Terry Blackman)

1993

In January the Board were told that the council were looking into the sale of Eastbourne Buses. The Government were contemplating legislation in the future making this compulsory, but to encourage councils to do so willingly, they were being allowed to keep 100 per cent of any receipts from such sales if completed by December 1993, other than the 50 per cent which would otherwise be allowed.

The possibility of predatory action from Stagecoach may well have had a bearing on the future value of the company to any prospective purchaser.

Management decided that the Board would be approached to see if they could spend up to £15,000 on a feasibility study. This was to be kept very confidential as it could do untold harm if the public found out about it.

The Board were informed by the MD, David Howard, that the Chief Executive had been instructed by the leader of the council to evaluate the assets of all departments with a view to helping with their financial crisis. The bus company had been included in this with a view to seeing whether it was worth considering its disposal.

An independent company had been engaged in order to ascertain the value of the bus company. This report was discussed in detail by the Bus Board which was unanimous in its view that high priority should be given to the future employment of the directors and staff, as well as to the travelling public, and that the interests of all concerned would be best met by the buses remaining under the control of the council. They felt a meeting with the Leader of the Council and the Chief Executive should be arranged to express their views.

The council came to the conclusion that unless they were forced to sell by the Government, then no further action would be taken.

This was to be the year of the company's ninetieth anniversary. On 12 April there was to be a re-enactment of the first-ever journey from the railway station to Meads. On 18 July the Eastbourne Omnibus Society staged a bus rally on the seafront. An anniversary dinner was also organised by the social club. The council were asked if they could supply a venue free of charge. Retired managers and staff were to be invited.

There would also be a staff outing to the Romney Hythe and Dymchurch Railway. This would coincide with the unveiling of one of the railway's diesel locomotives, painted in Eastbourne Buses livery. This locomotive had been spray-painted in the paint shops of Eastbourne Buses after being transported there on a low loader. I suspect a 'deal' had been brokered for this by the MD as the railway taught him how to drive one of their locos. This came

Volvo No.20. These were sweatboxes during the summer months and were the subject of many passenger complaints as they had no opening windows. (Terry Blackman)

in very handy for him a few years later, as he was to become MD of the Isle of Man's public transport, which included their steam railway system.

Eastbourne Buses also inaugurated a new bus route that terminated at New Romney station after serving many villages on the Kent/Sussex border on its way from Eastbourne. This service was never viable, but certainly made a pleasant change to operate as the round trip took the entire day and driving along country lanes made a pleasant break from town work.

The Government was considering putting VAT on bus fares. There was an EEC directive stating that this must be done before 1996 to bring the UK into line with other European countries. The difference was that most European countries heavily subsidised their public transport. In a report by the MD he suggested that fares might have to rise by 30–35 per cent to take into account the loss of patronage by a 17.5 per cent increase. He also thought there may have to be some service cuts. The cost of school services to councils would also increase. The Bus and Coach Council lobbied Parliament to have the proposed increases stopped.

1994

In February two new DAF Icaruses (116 and 117) were purchased.

The MD was asked by the Board to look into the viability of running a service that connected with the Newhaven–Dieppe ferry. He reported back that there were four sailings each way every day. Most of the users were car drivers. The railways ran a connecting train service, but this was not advertised as such. On average there were fewer than 100 foot passengers per sailing. To provide a connecting service for each sailing would cost £414 per day and he recommended that this would not be viable and was against proceeding with the scheme. There would also be problems if the ferry was delayed as the service would be timetabled to leave at a certain time and could not wait for the ferry, which really defeated the object of the service.

The Borough Council received permission to run a Dotto train along the road between the Sovereign Centre swimming pool at the east end of the town and the pier. This did not please David Howard who thought it unfair competition with the bus service. He compiled a report saying that the vehicle did not have to conform to the strict safety standards of PSV vehicles. Other UK bus and coach operators had shown concern over their use and the Bus and Coach Council were trying to seek clarity on whether they were legal. The Transport and General Workers Union had also protested to the Government over their use.

The MD also contacted the police stating that, as they were limited to a maximum speed of 10mph, this would lead to congestion. Unfortunately the police did not agree with him and the service started.

1995

Four new DAF Icaruses (28–31) were delivered. They were to prove very reliable vehicles and finished their lives on routes to Tunbridge Wells and East Grinstead.

At the start of the year the bus precinct, nicknamed 'Diesel Alley', hit the local headlines again, when a former Town Centre Manager suggested that the bus lanes should be pedestrianised and the buses moved elsewhere. His ideas met with mixed reactions with some café owners agreeing with him as they could then have Continental-style outside seating, whilst others thought that moving the buses would lose them trade. The problem with moving the bus stops was simply that there was nowhere suitable to move them to. David Howard MD was fairly uncommitted on the subject but said that any proposals should be carefully considered and he would be against any decision that would increase costs and if people wanted a reduction in engine fumes, then perhaps the number of private cars entering the town centre should be reduced. The local paper ended an article on the subject by saying that 'the overwhelming view was that the current situation is unsatisfactory. Diesel Alley must go.' In February a blueprint on the future aimed at easing congestion and improving public transport was published. This included proposals to move the bus precinct nearer to the station and the introduction of park-and-ride schemes. Needless to say, nothing changed – the bus precinct is still there and Eastbourne is no nearer a park-and-ride scheme.

Three bus drivers were chastised in the letters page in a local paper as they were sent to pick up a group of schoolchildren from a local theatre where they had been attending a forum on climate change. Whilst they were waiting for their passengers to come out, they left their engines running!

DAF No. 16 at Memorial Square roundabout in the town centre in an all-over advert for a new multi-use ticket, marketed as a '12 Card'. (Author's collection)

1996

An express bus service was introduced running between Eastbourne and Brighton. This was the service 30 and the dual-purpose vehicle, 27, was used for this service. It was always difficult making this service viable as it was in competition with a good rail service. It did build up a regular clientele of about thirty passengers, but long-term roadworks, which severely delayed the service on a daily basis, hastened its demise. The MD did request compensation from the County Council, but his request was denied.

In reply to a question from a local councillor about low-floor buses, David Howard responded that all buses purchased since 1990 had been equipped with DIPTAC features. There were still four buses that were the cause of complaint, but to equip these would cost £3,000 each. Two would be done as soon as funds permitted, but the other two were due for disposal.

He reported further that, ironically, the County Council normally accepts the lowest tender for their services and these are normally won by operators with older, less passenger-friendly vehicles.

The Government were contemplating making low-floor buses compulsory, but at that time they were expensive, mechanically unreliable and could seat fewer passengers and any reduction in the ability to move the numbers of foreign students that invade the town in the summer would adversely affect the company's ability to run an efficient service.

Another problem with passengers boarding and alighting was the lack of parking enforcement in the town, which meant buses could not get near the kerbs to load and unload. It was to be another twelve years before any effective parking enforcement in the town came into being.

The MD looked into whether EU grants could be obtained into converting buses to run on LPG or gas, but he discovered that they could not. There was an experiment about to start in Newcastle where electric buses were to be trialled and the MD reported he would keep an eye on the outcome.

1997

When the new timetable was released, the front cover showed a DAF that had been bought second-hand which was showing a destination number that did not match the destination. This brought two letters of derision in the local press saying that it did not exactly inspire confidence in the service.

In August a passenger complained that a gold ring that she had found and handed in would not be returned to her if was not claimed, but be given to the driver of the bus. Lost property legally belongs to the company and they can do with it as they wish if it is not claimed. Money received from claimed lost property was donated by the drivers to purchase equipment for the local hospital.

A radical plan to transform the town centre was adopted by the Eastbourne Borough Council in November. This included extending the Arndale Shopping Centre, lining the streets with trees and Victorian-style streetlights and, most radical of all, a tram service to replace the buses. The plans were the culmination of eighteen months' work by council officials. Questionnaires were sent out to traders and a firm of transport consultants employed. Needless to say, as Eastbourne does not do radical, none of these plans ever came to fruition. If only some of the money spent on plans, questionnaires and consultants was spent on actually doing things, Eastbourne could be a different place.

DAF No.25 in overall white livery as originally delivered in Terminus Road precinct. (Terry Blackman)

1998

In March, the company stopped running the service 30 from Brighton to Eastbourne via the A27. They had tried for about four years to make it profitable and had a regular clientele, but they were not enough to make it viable. The roadworks and good rail service finally led to its demise.

During the local elections in 1998, the Green Party candidate declared that he wanted to make Eastbourne Buses a publicly accountable trust, run for and accountable to local residents. He never expanded on quite how this would work and only got 224 votes, so like half the fleet on a very cold morning, it was a non-starter!

Police asked the company if their officers could travel free on the buses when on or off duty. David Howard readily agreed to this request and the crews are always happy to have an officer on board. The police were reported as saying it was 'masterminded' by a senior officer who had had the 'brainwave' when being short of police cars. Somewhat over the top, I thought.

Stagecoach and Guide Friday started a sightseeing tour that was competition to Eastbourne's service 3 open-top bus service to the top of Beachy Head. The tour also served the top but then returned through the town centre via Old Town before returning to the pier via the eastern end of the seafront.

You may be forgiven for thinking that after nearly 100 years of operation, there could be no new incidents, but you'd be wrong. In November a schoolgirl managed to get her arm caught in the back of a bus seat. She panicked which caused her arm to swell. The fire brigade had to be called, who released her using hydraulic equipment.

1999

The year did not start off too well with a headline ('Hell Ride') in the local paper above a report on the publication of a six-month survey on the buses. The report highlighted five major concerns: too few services to certain parts of the town; inadequate early-morning and evening services; poor Sunday services; not enough promotional fares; and lack of information

Twelve DAF Spectras lined up at Birch Road for a publicity shot soon after delivery. (Eastbourne Buses Ltd)

at bus stops. One Liberal Democrat councillor, Ron Parsons, said, 'We haven't got a bus service in Eastbourne. It's as simple as that.' The Chairman of the Eastbourne Buses Board, another Liberal Democrat councillor, Maurice Skilton, disagreed, saying the service in Eastbourne was second to none, with staff doing a tremendous job. A Tory councillor on the Board agreed with him, saying that they were in a competitive environment and that anyone could challenge Eastbourne Buses on the service it provided, but they didn't.

The headline in the paper brought a strong response in the letters page two weeks later. Even a lady who is renowned for writing to the paper complaining about the bus service sprang to its defence! Staff, including myself, also had letters published pointing out to Cllr Parsons that his party owned the Bus Company and had the power by law to improve off-peak and publicly desirable services, but chose not to. They were accused of using the buses as blatant electioneering as the local elections were approaching fast.

David Howard MD responded to the criticisms by announcing more Sunday services from May, as well as marketing initiatives to improve the usage of evening services. He also pointed out that the company had done well to survive the thirteen years since privatisation, as many municipally owned bus companies had been bought out.

The bus company was being blamed for businesses folding in the bus precinct, known as Diesel Alley. Three shops closed within three weeks and the buses were accused of being partly to blame. It seems strange to me that no-one complained before Terminus Road became buses only and the road was open to cars and lorries as well as the buses. David Howard responded by saying that alterations to the fleet had been carried out, low-sulphur fuel was now being used and the term Diesel Alley was now outdated.

At the AGM of Eastbourne Buses, an extraordinary event took place. Present were the two working directors, Mr David Howard MD and Miss Anne Clark (Financial Director), together with the four councillors – two Conservatives and two Liberal Democrats who made up the Board.

During the meeting Sari Conway (Eastbourne's Chief Executive) and the leader of the Liberal-controlled council, Cllr Bert Leggett, entered the meeting, halted the proceedings and made all those present sign deeds of confidentiality.

They then announced that they had been engaged in talks with a French company, Keolis, and they were going to sell part of the company.

None of the Board had any idea that this had been going on behind their backs and were not at all happy. Cllr Maurice Skilton was a well-respected Liberal councillor, who had served the town very well, and to be treated like this by the leader of his own party was, to my mind, appalling. Why the members present signed these confidentiality documents also puzzled me. I can understand why Liberal councillors did as their leaders told them, and maybe why the working directors did as their employers told them, but why should two Tory councillors sign?

Rumours at the depot were rife about a takeover by a French company but the staff were kept in the dark and were beginning to fear for their jobs. The local union officers wrote to the council asking for assurances that jobs and pensions would be safeguarded. These assurances were given.

A Tory councillor broke the news that 10–15 per cent of the company was to be sold to the French company, but there was no way the company as a whole would be sold.

In August, David Howard shocked the staff and council by handing in his notice. The staff knew that he was very unhappy with the way he had been treated by the council, who had been negotiating the possible sale of the company without including him.

The next step in the sales process was to set up a Steering Committee to discuss the details of the sale of shares. This committee was made up of the members of the bus board already mentioned, the leaders and deputy leaders of both political parties (forget Labour – this is Eastbourne we're talking about), officers from the council and two union representatives, including myself.

At the first meeting at the Town Hall, my colleague and I were asked to sign the same confidentiality documents as the councillors had. We refused point blank. We said it was our responsibility to keep our members informed, and we could not do this if we signed this document. After some discussion, it was decided that we would not have to sign, but may be requested to leave the meeting if a confidential matter arose. We accepted this.

As the meeting progressed, surprise was expressed at how certain senior members of the council seemed not to be acting in the best interests of everyone present. At one stage, the meeting was halted for nearly half an hour while the Chief Executive conducted a private discussion with the leader of the ruling party.

I then wrote a letter to the local paper regarding the sell-out, which evidently was not appreciated as I was removed from the Steering Committee. A Liberal councillor, with whom I had been mates for about twenty years, asked to meet me for a chat, but never turned up and refused to answer many requests for him to call me. When I bumped into him in a supermarket a while later, he told me he had been advised not to speak to me. A lot of misunderstanding would have been avoided if he had.

It was decided not to replace David Howard MD when he left but to allow the Finance Director to take the reins until the situation had become more settled.

In October the local paper printed an article claiming that four other companies had shown an interest in buying Eastbourne Buses. They were reported as being Metroline, Go-Ahead, Arriva and local firm RDH. Both RDH and Go-Ahead confirmed their interest, but the other two declined to comment.

Chapter 11

A New Century – The End of an Era

Sale of shares to Keolis; introduction of bus lanes; takeover of some routes from Stagecoach; Cavendish Motors start services; one-day strike; death of a driver; finances worsen

2000

In the wake of the previous year's events, where Sari Conway and the council leader had negotiated the sale of part of the company to Keolis, it would appear that relations between those at Town Hall and the Chief Executive remained strained, as she eventually offered to resign her post. As an investigation into alleged misconduct was in progress at the time, this offer was immediately rejected by councillors, though the Chief Executive was later relieved of her post after the conclusion of the council's proceedings.

However, the changes in the make-up of the council came too late for Eastbourne Buses Ltd and 20 per cent of the shares were sold to the French company Keolis for £462,000.

Although Keolis owned 20 per cent of the shares and had a seat on the Board, from the staff's and passengers' point of view, their presence did not seem to have made any difference.

One happy point in the year was a special fiftieth birthday party for the AEC Regal. The MOT bay was converted into a restaurant with hired dining tables and chairs. A gathering of existing and retired staff and managers, together with enthusiasts and supporters, witnessed a much-needed public relations exercise.

During the year, interviews were held for the post of Managing Director. The Tory Chairman of the Board, the Deputy Chief Executive of the Council and a Board member from Keolis were responsible for choosing a successor to David Howard. Steve Barnett was appointed. Steve was from Stagecoach and all future appointments to his management team were also ex-Stagecoach. Miss Clark, who had held the fort until Steve was appointed, was made redundant as the Board decided her post no longer existed, but the accountant who was brought in to replace her was eventually made a director himself.

Steve proved to be the last MD Eastbourne Buses had. Many people lay the demise of the company firmly at his door, but some major factors like the spiralling cost of insurance and fuel as well as competition were beyond his control.

2001

At the start of the year buses managed to demolish two bus shelters. Honours were even with Stagecoach destroying one at the pier and Eastbourne Buses knocking one over in the bus precinct.

Yet another scheme that never came to fruition was a plan to introduce bus lanes. Most towns had managed to introduce these, but not Eastbourne. Three or four sites were earmarked for a bus lane. It was then stated that the one that would be given priority would be alongside Seaside recreation ground on the approach to the traffic lights at Whitley Road. Was this because this was a particularly congested area? No. This was because it was not outside anybody's homes and there would be less opposition from locals, and then residents would be used to bus lanes and there would be less opposition in the future! However, residents opposite complained, enquiry after enquiry followed and seven or eight years and thousands of wasted pounds later, councillors finally abandoned the scheme!

A service taking clubbers home at 2.25a.m. was started. A pilot service that ran a few months earlier was scrapped due to lack of uptake. The new service was to be funded by four town centre clubs as part of the Community Safety Partnership and any profit would be shared among the clubs. After twelve weeks the number of passengers using the service was very low and the clubs stopped the funding and the service was scrapped.

More money was wasted by surveying 9,000 people who worked or studied in the District Hospital and adjacent colleges to ascertain where they lived by use of their postcode in a bid to improve services and persuade car users to switch to buses. The survey revealed that buses were not used because fares were too high, bus stops were inconveniently placed and buses needed to take a more direct route. A bus 'interchange' (simply a bus stop that can hold three buses!) was planned within the grounds of the hospital but this never materialised.

A group of business students also interviewed passengers on the buses to try to ascertain their movements. This survey was to be combined with the previously mentioned one to plan a new improved service for the town.

Yobs throwing stones at buses were becoming increasingly common, especially in the Langney area of the town. A decision was taken to withdraw all evening services from the area for a week, but with the threat of immediate withdrawal if any more incidents occurred.

Steve Barnett MD put forward controversial plans to rid the town of double-deckers. He said that these were only needed in the summer when the town had an influx of foreign students. The rest of the year the services were used mainly by the town's elderly population who found it difficult climbing stairs. He maintained that a crop of smaller vehicles would halve the time for the travelling public. With this in mind, in October 2001 a deal was signed with Reading Buses to exchange six of Eastbourne's Optare Spectras (276–281) for ten of their Excels (951–960). The Excels started arriving at the beginning of November. A taste of their unreliability occurred when one caught fire whilst being delivered.

2002

There was some good news for bus operators in the county at the start of the year with the announcement that a £363,000 grant from the Government's Rural Bus Challenge fund would be available. Most of the money went to rural services, but Eastbourne did benefit from the sale of combined train/bus tickets and the introduction of build-outs at bus stops. These builds-outs had three functions: to raise kerb levels to allow easier access to buses: to prevent illegal parking on bus stops: and to hinder traffic from passing so that when the bus was loaded it had a relatively clear road in front of it. This last one, however, does have a detrimental effect

One of the Excels that came from Reading, painted in a rather dull all-over blue livery. (Author's collection)

inasmuch that buses following each other relatively closely also get caught up with other traffic stuck behind buses loading at a stop.

In February Eastbourne Buses made use of the injection of cash from its sale of shares to Keolis by purchasing routes from Stagecoach. These routes consisted of a circular route that took in the villages of Stone Cross and Polegate and routes that went further north taking in the towns of Hailsham, Heathfield and Tunbridge Wells. Stagecoach closed its depot in Susans Road in the town centre and the site was subsequently sold for redevelopment.

The drivers that were displaced were taken on by Eastbourne Buses under TUPE (Transfer of Undertakings (Protection of Employment) arrangements.

Six DAF single-deckers were purchased (50–55). One of these, bus 55, was painted in gold livery to commemorate the Golden Jubilee of the Queen.

Mindless violence against the buses continued with a window being smashed by an air rifle bullet at 4p.m. on a June afternoon. Luckily none of the schoolchildren on board was injured. Later the same day a stone hurled at a bus smashed another window. Soon after the incidents the buses were pulled off the route to avoid any further incidents or injuries. Although a youth with a gun was seen running from the scene of the original attack, he was never caught.

Using all the information gleaned from the surveys undertaken in 2001, and with a great deal of influence from the new French part-owner, a new 'improved' service was announced to start in September. Most of the services were completely altered with new services serving areas of the town that until then had never enjoyed a service. Circular routes which had served the town's 'polo mint' shape were replaced by feeder services to hubs. The staff were not happy with the changes and one driver leaked to the press that morale at the depot was low, with agreements with management being broken, timetables for the new services being printed very late and predicting chaos with the introduction of the new services.

The staff's concerns were soon followed by howls of protest from passengers, with the changes described as 'horrendous' with many people having to use two buses rather than one

Northern Counties-bodied DAF in Queen's Golden Jubilee livery pictured in Meadow Road,
Tunbridge Wells, on service 52. (Author's collection)

to complete their journeys and other people claiming they would have to give up jobs as they
could not reach work on time without leaving their schoolchildren alone.

One passenger's frustrations led to her being thrown off the bus by police. She refused to
pay her fare complaining that her bus was always late or failed to turn up. When she became
abusive, the police were called and she was removed from the bus. On the day in question, the
bus she was waiting for had broken down and the following bus was late.

At another estate in the town a driver had to be rushed to hospital with glass in his eye after
a missile had been hurled through his cab window. Two days later on the same estate, a hooligan
deliberately threw a live firework rocket at a bus. This resulted in the buses being immediately
withdrawn from the area and they were not reinstated until a week later. Steve Barnett MD
told the press that if the attacks continued, the estate would lose its service permanently.

At the end of the year I made front-page headlines in the *Eastbourne Herald*. I was driving the
rear-entry Leyland PD2, No.82, with a clippie on the back, and we had to go to Willingdon
School on the last day of term to take the pupils home. Two or three of them emerged from
the school covered in flour. I warned the kids that if the bus was vandalised, I would be taking
them back to the depot. About 10 minutes into the journey, I received a rapid series of bells
from the clippie. Unable to see her in the interior mirror, I stopped the bus and went round
the back and upstairs to see the floor of the upper saloon covered in flour. I thought my clippie
could be next in line for a flour bomb so true to my word, I diverted the bus back to the depot,
found a mop and bucket and told them we would not be going any further until they had
cleared up the mess. After a few insults came my way, they realised I meant what I said, and the
bus was duly cleaned. We continued the journey. Some parents were not happy that their little
darlings were late home and one man even contacted the police to claim that I had kidnapped
his daughter. The police did visit the depot, but never caught up with me personally, so does
this mean I am still on the run?! Amazingly, the company backed me up and I never heard any
more about it.

2003

This was the centenary of the bus company. A special event called Eastbourne Motorbus 100 was organised with the help of the East Sussex Omnibus Society. The usual commemorative run was made, following in the wheel tracks of the original service from the town centre to Meads. Three vehicles took part in this and seats were reserved for invited guests. The vehicles involved were the privately preserved ex-Eastbourne No.12 Leyland Lion, the AEC Regal No.11 and the latest addition to the fleet, DAF No.55 in gold livery. The Pilot public house in Meads was used for a buffet.

At the end of the financial year, the company had made a loss of £199,785, but this figure included an exceptional write-off of stock of £57,000. This followed losses in 2001 of £73,375 and 2002 of £179,075.

The acquisition of the new country routes from Stagecoach had largely been responsible for a 10 per cent increase in turnover, but this improvement was wiped out by a 15 per cent increase in overheads.

The Directors though did predict better things for the future. The Company forecasted a profit of £180,000 for 2004 and for 2005 forecasted a further increase in profit to £251,000. I think they forgot to mention that these figures had been compiled using their rose-coloured spectacles.

The council were happy not to receive a dividend on their investment. Instead it was understood that Eastbourne Buses would operate socially desirable, but unprofitable services that would otherwise be put out to tender.

2004

The local communities of Westham and Pevensey organised themselves and with the help of officers of East Sussex County Council applied to the Transport Rural Bus Challenge for a grant under the Kickstart programme. The first attempt was unsuccessful, but they tried again and this time succeeded in obtaining a grant of £533,600. The funding was to last for three years. The service started on Monday 26 July.

A movie was made and distributed on DVD called *Rover 6 The Movie*. The Rover 6 was billed as 'the bus that comes when you call'. It was a low-floor bus with a ramp, and it ran every day except Sunday, taking passengers shopping, to the doctors and as a direct transfer for the service 5, thus linking with Eastbourne. To use Rover 6, you simply rang the Travel Centre at least an hour before you needed the bus.

A competition was run to name the buses and these were named *Marshmallow, Westham Flyer, Pevensey Leveller, Andereida, Norman Rover* and *Roman Rover*.

They were given a distinctive livery, equipped with CCTV cameras and banned from being used on any other routes.

The buses used were DAF SB120s (56–61), but badged as Volvos. I believe Volvo had been having problems developing a new low-floor bus and had bought some from DAF and sold them under their name.

This led to a problem as a few weeks into the new service, a fuel pipe ruptured and the fuel was sprayed under high pressure all over the hot engine causing it to burst into flames. The driver managed to get all the passengers safely from the vehicle but the rear of the bus was very badly damaged. This led to a legal wrangle as to which of the manufacturers was responsible for repairing the bus and it was over a year before the bus returned to service.

In the first six months the Rover 6 provided approximately 3,000 passenger journeys. The service 5 provided 122,000 journeys in the same period.

Lost property that is claimed from the bus depot is returned to its owners on payment of £1. This should be returned to the driver who handed it in, but fifteen years previously, the drivers decided to donate their monies to charity. On hearing that the local hospital's Special Baby Care Unit was in need of a state-of-the-art breast pump to help mothers who were having difficulty in producing milk, £995 was donated from the lost property fund to buy one.

2005

Eastbourne Buses took over the operation of the Dotto train, which had been operated by the council for fifteen years along the length of the seafront. There were two trains each pulling three carriages – there had been three, but one was written off in a fire in the previous year. Eastbourne Buses agreed to pay £30,000 to the council for the right to operate the train and pay all the running costs themselves. They would keep all the income, but if the profit from the operation rose above £25,000 any income would be shared on a 50-50 basis. This deal absolved the council of any financial risk and a deal was agreed.

Evening bus services were suspended to an estate at the eastern end of the town following more attacks on the buses, including shots being fired at the vehicles with an air gun. I was working one evening, and was flagged down by a driver coming the other way on the estate, who informed me I would probably be shot at further up the road!

It seemed a bit surreal as I drove along waiting to be shot. I reached the end of the road and breathed a sigh of relief as I thought I had made it safely, when there was a loud crack and a side window shattered. I don't know what I was thinking but I pulled up round the corner, left the bus and tried to creep up on the gunman. Luckily it started raining and I thought that although I didn't mind risking being shot at, there was no way I was going to get wet as well, so I returned to the bus! What I did not realise was that an inspector had been following me in an unmarked car and had seen the culprit firing from a bedroom window. The police were called and a young lad arrested. It turned out that his parents had gone out and he was bored and claimed that he was aiming his airgun at a lamppost rather than the bus. Under our wonderful legal system, I was classified as a victim and could have a say in his punishment. Thinking that the punishment should fit the crime, I thought that he should spend a day cleaning the buses, rather than destroying them. The authorities agreed to this and said this would happen within the next YEAR! Why so long? Needless to say, he was never made to serve his punishment. This was not the only incident on the estate and buses still do not serve some roads in the evening.

The Green Party was still dissatisfied with the way that services were being run in the town. They suggested that the bus service should be run by a trust. Their spokesman said that there are now hundreds of examples of publicly accountable independent trusts running all kinds of former local authority and other services on behalf of the communities they serve. Public transport services should be there for the benefit of the public and to offer an affordable, reliable, safe and more environmentally friendly way of getting around. Eastbourne Greens want to see more services and an extended local bus network in Eastbourne alongside the introduction of a cheap 'flat fare' scheme to encourage more people to switch to buses for journeys around town. Trust status would allow Eastbourne Buses to take full advantage of all Government subsidies or grants available and ensure that every penny is invested into improved services for local residents. Needless to say that this idea was not taken up.

On 17 August a mechanic was seriously injured at the depot. He was working on his own refitting an engine to an ex-Reading Excel. The engine was suspended on a trolley and he was lying beneath it. The trolley toppled over crushing the poor guy. He was fortunate inasmuch as very soon after the accident a delivery driver entered the depot and it was he who raised the alarm. He suffered broken ribs and damage to his right lung and heart muscle and was in a coma for some days. Two fitters had decoupled the gearbox from the engine and took it away to work on it separately. He then lay down under the engine to replace a hose that had previously been removed and, as he got up, the trolley tipped up and the engine fell on him, pinning him to the floor. He spent six weeks in hospital, three of them in intensive care, and will never work again.

Health and Safety Executive Inspector Andrew Christian stated that separating the two parts of the power pack had unbalanced the load on the trolley. He went on:

> If you take the large lump of a gearbox off one end, you are obviously going to change the centre of gravity. It's likely that having replaced the hose, he added his weight just to pull himself up. And if you add another 80 kilos to one end, it would be enough to cause it to overbalance.

Hove Crown Court heard that the company had no risk assessment for splitting the power pack and that, though the sixty-one-year-old mechanic was an experienced engineer, he had received no training on the type of engine he was working on that day. Eastbourne Buses were subsequently fined £25,000 with costs of £12,725 for the accident.

2006

Cavendish Motor Services started operating services in Eastbourne on 13 March under the name of The Lighthouse Line. This was a joint venture between ex-Managing Director David Howard and Christian Harmer, the owner of local coach operator Renown Coaches. David Howard had recently retired from being in charge of all the public transport systems on the Isle of Man. He had kept his house in the village of Pevensey, just outside Eastbourne.

Many people thought that he had entered this venture partly as revenge on Eastbourne Council over the way he had been treated by the council when he was MD. The service started with two routes: No.10, which crossed the town in an east-west direction; and No.11 which served Hailsham by a different route to that used by Eastbourne Buses.

David Howard ran this on the same business lines as he probably would have done with Eastbourne Buses had he been given the chance, with the buses not hitting the road until about 8a.m. and no service in the evenings or Sundays. They undercut the fares charged by Eastbourne Buses, having a flat fare of £1 or 50p for old-age pensioners.

They used single-deck buses and used a very good public relations exercise by using the old Southdown livery of green and cream.

They also purchased a Routemaster, which was also painted in their livery and subsequently named 'David R. Howard'.

In July the members of the TGWU voted to hold two one-day strikes in support of a pay claim. Although the pay rates were lower than those of the Brighton and Hove drivers operating from our depot, many staff voted for action as a protest against the way two Operations Managers had been treating them over the last few years and the pay rates were a secondary consideration.

Bearing in mind that only just over half the drivers had returned their ballot papers and only just over half of them voted to strike, the turnout on the picket lines was very good with over 80 per cent of the staff doing a turn on the picket lines during the first day, Thursday 15 June. About five buses did leave the depot and these were used on school contract work. The attitude of the strikers was very good-natured. When I stood in front of one of the disliked managers' cars to stop him entering the depot, he literally started pushing me out of the way with his front bumper. I complained to one of the police officers that he was trying to run me over. The sympathetic officer replied, 'Get out of the way then!'

During the day, preliminary talks were held with management, and the second day's strike was called off. Since then, we've had a better Operations Manager, and it became a far better place to work.

On 4 September a fatal accident occurred at the Birch Road depot, when Driver Roy Trundell, sixty-two, was tragically killed by a reversing bus. He had just driven into the yard and parked his bus directly behind another bus. He left his cab and walked between his bus and the one parked in front just as the latter was reversing. The driver of the reversing bus had boarded his bus before Roy had arrived and did not expect another vehicle to be directly behind him. Indeed it was not visible in his mirrors. Unfortunately Roy was trapped between the two buses and crushed.

Roy was a well-liked, jovial chap who started his bus-driving career in London. His funeral at the local crematorium was packed to overflowing and his former colleagues from London attended in a Routemaster with a destination blind suitably made in memorial to Roy. The town's buses came to a standstill at 3.15p.m., the time of Roy's funeral, to begin a 2-minute silence.

The subsequent inquest returned a verdict of accidental death and the police also concluded that it was a tragic accident and never brought any charges.

This accident led to an investigation by the Health and Safety Executive (HSE) and both the company and the Managing Director, Steve Barnett, facing charges. The verdict of accidental death did not deter the HSE from pursuing Eastbourne Buses Ltd.

It did lead to a tightening up of safety procedures at the depot, not that they were terribly lax before. In my view, Roy's death was a freak accident with many contributory factors, none of which were dangerous alone, but in combination, proved fatal.

What annoyed me and many other employees at the depot was that while the HSE were pursuing us, Cavendish Motors were operating from a piece of wasteland with no overhead lighting, no lane markings, no one way systems within the yard and no requirement to wear high-visibility clothing, yet despite complaints to the HSE they seemed very reluctant to do anything about it. Indeed when I was inspecting our yard with a HSE inspector, who in my opinion was nit-picking saying that this stop line could be moved by about 3ft and that another notice could be put on this door, he refused point blank to discuss Cavendish's yard. I would have thought their main objective should be to prevent accidents rather than spend hundreds of hours and thousands of pounds pursuing a company that had a very good safety culture.

The subsequent sale of Cavendish Motors and closure of the yard means that we will never know if the HSE would have ever got their act together. In my opinion, their yard should have been shut down.

In December, the company was again in trouble with the HSE and were served with four enforcement notices as, in their words, 'Arrangements have not been made or given effect as are appropriate for the effective planning, organisation, control, monitoring and review of measures necessary to manage vehicle safety.' The company complied with the notices by the end of the following month.

On 25 June 2009 both Steve Barnett and Eastbourne Buses Ltd were found guilty of causing the death of Roy Trundell. Steve Barnett was fined £5,000 and the company £100,000.

The judge said that although the company were not putting profit before safety, they had not caught up with health and safety matters. The company, by then owned by Stagecoach, changed its plea during the trial from not guilty to guilty.

Steve Barnett continued to maintain his innocence by claiming he had delegated responsibility for risk assessment and daily health and safety to his managers. Costs of £5,000 and £135,000 were awarded against Steve Barnett and Eastbourne Buses respectively.

2007

In July, the funding for the service 5 and Rover 6 finished. The service as a whole was not profitable and it finished, although parts of the service 5 route managed to survive the cuts.

David Howard, the former managing director of Eastbourne Buses who went on to found Cavendish Motors, sadly died suddenly of a heart attack. His funeral took place at St Nicolas Church in Pevensey and was attended by 200 family members, friends and colleagues from the transport industry.

On 29 September, a free bus service was organised along Eastbourne's seafront to commemorate David Howard's life using the Cavendish Routemaster, Eastbourne Buses Regal No.11, ex-Eastbourne Lion No.12, JK 8418 and Ensigns RLH61.

The two accidents in the depot had had a very bad effect on the health of the MD Steve Barnett and he was having long periods off sick. The Board persuaded ex-MD Roger Bowker, who had retired from full-time employment with Stagecoach, to come back temporarily to run the company.

On 28 November, Eastbourne Buses Ltd were called to appear before the Traffic Commissioner at a Public Inquiry following a report from the Vehicle and Operator Services Agency (VOSA) which alleged that the company failed to operate bus services in accordance with its registered particulars. VOSA monitors presented evidence of bus services that did not run to timetable or did not run at all.

Bus Compliance Officer Cheetham's evidence concluded that of the bus services observed, 160 out of 206 observations ran within the window of tolerance. Forty-two journeys were more than 5 minutes late in departing from their timing point and four journeys departed more than 1 minute early. The overall non-compliance rate was, therefore, 22–23 per cent.

The commissioner also considered a conviction that the company incurred when it was in breach of the Health and Safety at Work Act following an incident in which one of its fitters was injured. The company was fined £25,000 plus costs. Also under consideration was whether the company satisfied the requirement to be of appropriate financial standing.

The Company demonstrated it did have enough funds to continue trading, but was fined for failing to reach the required levels of operational performance and was hit with a fine that it really could have done without. This was £200 per bus amounting to a total of £14,000. The maximum fine that could have been imposed was £38,500. It does seem to be counterproductive to fine bus companies that are in financial difficulties, as the money paid in fines could be better spent improving the fleet, thereby improving reliability.

The commissioner does have the power to revoke, curtail or suspend an operator's licence. The 'window' for being on time is between 1 minute early and 5 minutes late. Although there is no excuse for running early, there are many reasons for running late. How many people who drive a car to work arrive at the same time every day? This is without the added problem of having to pick up and set down differing numbers of passengers. The fact that a company can get fined or lose its licence for running late can put undue pressure on drivers to keep on time, so I would question the fact that this is a sensible law. Obviously giving enough running time to cope with unforeseen hold-ups is one answer, but that would mean on days when everything runs smoothly, buses would have to stop and needlessly waste time and I know from experience that this annoys passengers.

The commissioner said that he had taken into account the manager's submissions that on the day in question the weather was bad and that some of the late runnings were the same bus being booked on both the outward and return journeys, when it could not have picked up the late running time in the short period that it was booked.

The Optare Excels were withdrawn from Eastbourne during 2007 and sold to South Gloucestershire Bus and Coach, owned by Rotala. They were so unreliable that a couple of mechanics travelled with the convoy of buses when they were delivered, and a huge sigh of relief was breathed when they all made it without incident.

They were replaced by ten new MANs (62–71). The company could ill-afford to pay the increased lease costs, but it was hoped that these leasing costs would add up to less than the combined costs of leasing the Excels and paying for their maintenance. The increased reliability would also have increased financial benefits.

The company also realised that they would have to replace the ageing double-deckers with low-floor examples. There was no way that new doubles could be afforded and second-hand vehicles were few and far between. A company in Manchester, GM, formerly UK North, had been shut down by the authorities. This followed several accidents, one fatal. A subsequent investigation found that out of its 130 drivers, 100 were Polish who could hardly speak any English and were poorly trained. Eastbourne Buses bought four of their fleet (401–404), even though they knew the buses had been very badlly maintained.

Roger Bowker said that he wanted all these buses on the road by the end of the year. Looking at the state of the vehicles, most of us thought that this deadline was somewhat ambitious to say the least, as the workshops were struggling to keep the present fleet in a roadworthy condition without all this extra work. We were proved correct with only one bus, 401, making it into service that year.

Eastbourne Buses had made losses for the last seven years and the balance sheet was not healthy, to say the least. The finances were being attacked from many angles, spiralling fuel costs, insurance premiums going through the roof as well as having to pay fines for late running and Health and Safety, while income was suffering from the competition from Cavendish and income from concessionary fares dropping. East Sussex County Council did not subsidise any bus routes in Eastbourne – they were all run commercially. This had long been a bone of contention with the workforce, who saw many evening services in neighbouring Hastings run by Stagecoach being paid for by the ratepayers, but the same ratepayers saw no benefit in Eastbourne. Many staff thought that local councillors had one eye on the ballot box and feared upsetting their constituents and losing their seat at the next elections. This was one reason why decisions should have been made on a purely commercial basis.

The situation could not continue to deteriorate and the management informed the council that they could no longer afford to run service 51 in the evenings between Eastbourne and Hailsham from the end of September. Councils have the right to award contracts worth under £7,500 to companies under a *de minimis* arrangement without having to put services out to tender. The council decided that they could afford to pay this amount to Eastbourne Buses if they terminated two other poorly used services, namely an afternoon trip on non-schooldays between Lewes and Hailsham and an evening service from the Conquest Hospital in Hastings. This was done and the evening Hailsham service continued.

A review of the concessionary fares scheme was on hold pending the resolution of appeals by the Department for Transport. Any change to the scheme at this point, without the resolution of those appeals, would have resulted in further appeals. Bus companies wanted an increase in the amount they were reimbursed by East Sussex County Council for giving pensioners and the disabled free travel. Raising the reimbursement rate to 62.5 per cent would have added another £250,000 to the amount that would have to come from the rate fund. It was finally agreed to raise the percentage to 57.4 per cent.

2008

During the year the other three ex-Manchester buses made it into service, but one, 404, blew its engine after only about two weeks in service. The company could not afford to buy a replacement engine and this languished at the back of the workshop until funds became available.

The case brought against the firm following the death of an employee was heard at a Magistrates Court but the magistrates said they felt the matter was not within their jurisdiction and asked for it to be dealt with at Crown Court. It was not heard until 2009.

On 5 May I was called up to the MD's office with the other shop steward where we were introduced to the Liberal Chairman of the Board. We were advised that the two Conservative members of the Board had resigned. We were also informed that Keolis wished to sell their 20 per cent share of the company back to the council. The council though did not want to buy them back and had decided to put their 80 per cent on the market as well. He said there were already two interested parties. The chairman did state that he would prefer the buses to stay in their own livery. We knew Go-Ahead might allow this, but Stagecoach would not.

The chairman stated that they did not want Renown Cavendish to buy the company and thought it was OK to take the best offer from two bidders. He said there were two interested parties and did not deny they were Stagecoach and Go-Ahead.

Later on we learnt that Rotala and Arriva had shown an interest, but they dropped out as negotiations continued.

Most of the staff favoured a buyout from Go-Ahead as they also owned Brighton and Hove who had an outstation at our depot, had a modern fleet and had a better reputation towards their staff. I wrote to every councillor in Eastbourne stating this point of view. This letter was leaked to the local press who printed it.

Unfortunately our views were ignored probably because when the sealed bids were opened, there was a large difference in the offers and money was a major factor in the decision, so Stagecoach were successful. Their offer of over £4 million was more than anyone expected and with the promise of twelve new buses in January, together with a promise of no redundancies for road staff and mechanics, this was an offer that could not be refused.

Stagecoach's success led to a very interesting first meeting between me and a very senior Stagecoach executive who had seen my letter printed in the local paper saying that I'd rather work for one of their competitors!

17 December was the date of the last bus operated by Eastbourne Buses Ltd. The two directors left the depot at 4.30p.m. to go to the Town Hall to hand in their resignations, although they were to stay employed by Stagecoach until the New Year. The last bus ran in off service at about 11.30a.m. Six hours later a new chapter in Eastbourne's buses began when the first Stagecoach-operated service left the depot.

2009

You may wonder why there is an entry under 2009. Well Stagecoach took over and started turning us into one of their depots – new uniforms, buses being resprayed, and so on – when the Office of Fair Trading (OFT) stepped in and said they were launching an investigation. This was triggered because Stagecoach announced that they had also purchased Cavendish Motors and were going to integrate the two companies. This meant that they had a monopoly from East Kent, right along the coast to Eastbourne.

Early morning in December 2008
at Birch Road depot. (Phil Clarke)

Eleven out of the twelve new
Enviros lined up at Birch Road
depot. (Phil Clarke)

A Cadet at Uckfield bus station.
This was one of the few buses
repainted from the Eastbourne
livery before the Office of Fair
Trading stopped any further
repainting until they had finished
their investigations. (Author's
collection)

The OFT stopped Stagecoach from further integration whilst they were carrying out their investigation, unless they had their specific consent. This meant that no further buses could be sprayed in Stagecoach livery and further constraints put on further integration.

When Stagecoach took over the maintenance of the ex-Cavendish fleet, many of the buses were found to be un-roadworthy and were taken out of service. Initially some Eastbourne buses could be seen on ex-Cavendish routes until Stagecoach buses could be brought in from other depots to ease the situation. The two services were combined, without too much detriment to the travelling public.

Cavendish had been started because their management believed that, due to the poor financial situation, it was only a matter of time before Eastbourne Buses folded and they would become the major operator in the town. They had made an offer to the council to buy Eastbourne Buses, but their offer had been turned down.

Cavendish had increased their services to make it more attractive to a potential purchaser. However, the overriding concern behind its strategy was to protect Renown, and it could not have continued operating at its autumn 2008 level indefinitely. This strategy had been a risk, as it had not known how long Eastbourne Buses would continue for and that it would in the end have been allowed to fold.

When it became apparent to them that a major operator would be taking over Eastbourne Buses, they knew they would not be able to compete. Eastbourne Buses did not have the financial ability to compete with Cavendish on fares, but a major operator could destroy them, so the decision to sell their business was the best, and probably only, option.

One fact that was brought to light by the OFT was that a deal to buy Cavendish's shares was done in November 2008, before the deal to buy Eastbourne Buses had been finalised, even though the deal was not concluded until the new year. What also came to light was that Renown had contacted Brighton and Hove in March 2008. The original offer was to sell both Cavendish and Renown as separate entities, but it quickly became clear that Brighton and Hove were not interested in Renown. This was not a problem as the two companies were being operated as separate entities and Renown could continue trading using its core business of council contracts and school trips.

Renown initially accepted an offer for Cavendish, but Go-Ahead decided not to proceed with the deal. Renown believed that Go-Ahead would have come back to the negotiating table if it had purchased Eastbourne Buses.

Renown then approached Stagecoach when it was made known that Go-Ahead was not going to proceed with the purchase. They presumed that Stagecoach was bidding for Eastbourne Buses but were not aware of any details. The deal agreed with Stagecoach was very similar to that agreed with Go-Ahead, although there were some minor differences with regard to the treatment of assets. Stagecoach had taken a risk in paying a deposit to purchase Cavendish without confirmation that it also had acquired Eastbourne Buses. But Stagecoach could not lose as it could have sold Cavendish to the eventual buyers of Eastbourne or put its resources behind Cavendish and carried on competing. Renown knew that there were many different outcomes, but it was fairly confident that Stagecoach would have gone through with the purchase of Cavendish.

The OFT finished their deliberations and decided that the situation was serious enough to refer it to the Competition Commission.

The reason for this referral was that, given the absence of any evidence of likely entry in the short- to medium-term by other bus operators, there was a concern that the acquisitions could result in higher prices and/or decreased service quality to Eastbourne bus users.

In October, the Competition Commission finally published its conclusions, and to many people's amazement found that there was no case to answer. They thought that Cavendish's services were making losses that were not sustainable so they would withdraw their operation within Eastbourne, leaving Eastbourne Buses with a monopoly again. They therefore concluded that there would be no difference if Stagecoach had the monopoly.

Any driver from either company could have told them that Cavendish were not making money. Many of their services were running empty or nearly empty. Why did this take highly paid civil servants so long to work out? The cost to the taxpayer for this farce was £229,254.75!

Stagecoach were then free to continue their operation in Eastbourne with no constraints on future fares or routes.

EASTBOURNE BUSES R.I.P.